# LEADERSHIP
## FOR THE
# FUTURE

Drawing by Anthony: © 1988
The New Yorker Magazine, Inc.

# LEADERSHIP
## FOR THE
# FUTURE

*Changing Directorial Roles
in American History Museums
and Historical Societies*

Collected Essays

edited by

Bryant F. Tolles, Jr.
with a
Historical Prologue
by
Edward P. Alexander

**American Association for State and Local History**
Nashville, Tennessee

Published by the American Association for State and Local History, an international non-profit membership organization. For membership information, please contact Director of Membership Services, (615) 255-2971.

95 94 93 92 91 — 5 4 3 2 1


**Library of Congress Cataloging-in-Publication Data**

Leadership for the future : changing directorial roles in American
  history museums and historical societies : collected essays / edited
  by Bryant F. Tolles, Jr. with a historical prologue by Edward P.
  Alexander.
     p.  cm.
  ISBN 0-942063-11-2
     1. Museum directors—United States.   2. Historical museums—United
  States—Administration.   3. United States—History, Local—
  Societies, etc.—Administration.   4. United States—History, Local—
  Societies, etc.—Employees.   I. Tolles, Bryant Franklin, 1939–
  II. Alexander, Edward P. (Edward Porter), 1907–
  E172.L4  1991
  069.5025 '73—dc20                                              91–490
                                                                   CIP

# Contents

# Acknowledgments

I would like to thank my secretary, Mary Tabinowski, for word-processing and preparation of the manuscript. In addition, I would like to thank Edward P. Alexander for his willingness to read and edit the essays and contribute the historical prologue for this book. My further appreciation is due Clement M. Silvestro who also read and critiqued the manuscript.

Grateful acknowledgment for permission to use the illustrations goes to the following:

Adirondack Museum, Blue Mountain Lake, New York (p. 72)

Anthony: © 1988, The New Yorker Magazine, Inc., New York, New York (Frontispiece)

Chicago Historical Society, Chicago, Illinois (p. 28)

John Curry Archives, State of Michigan, Lansing, Michigan (p. 156)

DuSable Museum of African American History, Chicago, Illinois (p. 168)

Essex Institute, Salem, Massachusetts (p. 106)

Henry Ford Museum and Greenfield Village, Dearborn, Michigan (p. 22)

Chuck Kidd, Old Sturbridge Village, Sturbridge, Massachusetts (p. 146)

Massachusetts Historical Society, Boston, Massachusetts (p. 84)

Mercer Museum of the Bucks County Historical Society, Doylestown, Pennsylvania (p. 64)

John Miller Documents, Rhode Island Historical Society, Providence, Rhode Island (p. 122)

Monmouth County Historical Association, Freehold, New Jersey (p. 184)

Museum of the City of New York, New York, New York (p. 36)

Museums at Stony Brook, Stony Brook, New York (p. 136)

New York State Historical Association, Cooperstown, New York (pp. 48–49)

Old Salem Restorations, Winston–Salem, North Carolina (p. 98)

Pennsylvania Academy of Fine Arts, Philadelphia, Pennsylvania (p. 4)

# Preface

This collection of essays had its origins in a one-day conference—"Museum Leadership: Styles and Structures for the Future"—held in spring 1986 at the University of Delaware under the cosponsorship of the Museum Studies Program and the graduate student Museum Studies Association. The primary outgrowth of this event was the perceived need to direct more extensive as well as intensive attention in published form to the conference theme, specifically as it applies to chief executive officer (directorial) leadership in history museums, historical societies, and associated historical organizations in the United States. During the summer of 1986 I made initial contacts with the American Association for State and Local History concerning publication prospects and options, and inspired by the supportive guidance of Gerald George, former director of the association, and Candace Floyd, former assistant director and publications coordinator, the concept behind this volume was nurtured, became securely rooted, and over the ensuing two years gradually germinated. More recently, under the enthusiastic and competent guidance of current AASLH assistant director for publication services, Joanne Jaworski, the final details have been accomplished, and the book is now a pleasant reality.

While they speculate on the challenges and demands of the twenty-first century, the essays comprising LEADERSHIP FOR THE FUTURE also trace the quite dramatic change that has occurred in the nature of historical agency executive leadership over the past two decades. The role of director has become increasingly complex, taxing, and oftentimes burdensome, calling for broader vision, knowledge, social consciousness, commitment, energy, experience, fiscal and development acumen, and general management skills than ever before. The movement toward greater professionalism continues to progress as more and more the leadership in our nation's historical institutions takes on characteristics traditionally associated with the profit sector of American life. Where is this trend taking us? At this point one can only conjecture, as the contributors to this volume do. We know, though, that institutional heads are paying increasing attention to modern-day leadership concepts and principles of organizational management as they go about their important work. Before we examine, however, the present status of executive leadership at American history museums and historical societies and ponder their current condition and future needs with our essay authors, briefly let us glance back twenty years or so and reflect on how our specifications and expectations for leadership have changed.

As recently as the sixties the primary qualifications for successful museum leadership were viewed in terms that markedly contrast with today. Those active in museums then were more likely to regard training and demonstrated competency in a particular academic discipline, well-honed curatorial skills, broad knowledge of one's institutional collections, and, not insignificantly, impressive personal presence and polished social graces, as the primary requisites for leadership. But during the decade of the seventies a series of historical circumstances combined to bring about major change. Along came new state and federally funded grant programs, new corporate support programs for non-profits, the AAM accreditation and assessment processes, the national bicentennial commemoration, new federal tax and labor laws, and most significantly, rampant national inflation which stressed endowments and forced many institutions into greater reliance on improved fiscal administration and expanded earned income initiatives as they pursued "bottom line" operational objectives. In addition, in response to increasingly diversified public audiences, there has been a movement in history museums toward greater educational outreach and social responsibility. New theories and approaches to historical interpretation have challenged such institutions to serve their constituencies effectively, and yet, continue to present "a sophisticated and critical view of the past," through the use of their collections.[1]

What has the result been? We have witnessed a growing emphasis on effective, responsible, and responsive leadership and management for American museums, with much borrowed, philosophically as well as practically, from business enterprise. It is the above group of developments, spread out over a wide time frame, that has served to alter our perspectives of successful museum leadership, and the characteristics and skills required to achieve it. When selecting future museum leaders, therefore, today's boards of trustees are focusing on personal qualities—abilities to reason, communicate, persuade, facilitate, cultivate, challenge, inspire, and exercise vision—as well as learned and practiced expertise in such areas as long-range planning, resource development, finance, marketing, the law, professional standards, collections care and management, collections presentation and interpretation, facilities and security administration, and personnel management. Conditions, both internally and externally produced, have dictated that leadership in our museums must reach a higher level of professionalism, and indeed more professional we are becoming.

Following a comprehensive, stage-setting historical prologue by Edward P. Alexander, fifteen representatives of the historical agency field, all of them current or former chief executives, present their views on the essence, substance, and requirements of top-level leadership.

Each has been assigned a specific subject area appropriate to his or her strengths, talents, interests, and accomplishments. The resulting mosaic of philosophical impressions, theoretical observations, historical reflections, institutional case references, practical information, and nuggets of sound advice asks and answers some important questions about leadership, present and future, at American history museums and historical societies. At the same time, other questions are advanced about the field that await broader reflection and resolution in the years ahead. If this volume can partially accomplish the goal of provoking discussion about these questions, I and my distinguished list of colleagues will consider it an unqualified success.

Bryant F. Tolles, Jr.
Newark, Delaware
Spring, 1991

# LEADERSHIP
## FOR THE
# FUTURE

# Historical Prologue
# The Rise of American History Museums

by

## Edward P. Alexander

EDWARD P. ALEXANDER received an undergraduate degree from Drake University, and graduate degrees from the State University of Iowa (M.A.) and Columbia University (Ph.D.) in American history. He served as director of both the New York State Historical Association and the State Historical Society of Wisconsin, and then as director of interpretation at Colonial Williamsburg, where he established the Williamsburg Seminar for Historical Administration. In 1972 he was the first director of the Museum Studies Program at the University of Delaware, and is now professor emeritus of Museum Studies there. He has been president of the American Association for State and Local History and of the American Association of Museums. Since his retirement he has written two books and several articles on the history of museums.

*The Artist in His Museum,* 1822. Self-portrait by Charles Willson Peale (1741–1827). Gift of Mrs. Sarah Harrison (The Joseph Harrison, Jr., Collection). Courtesy of the Pennsylvania Academy of Fine Arts, Philadelphia, Pennsylvania.

*M*useums devoted to history comprise more than one-half of the over seven thousand museums in this country. They have evolved during the last two centuries from independent and state-supported historical societies, state historical departments, historic house museums, regular indoor museums, and outdoor or open-air museums. Many of them are more meagerly financed than their cousins in the fields of art, natural history, or science and technology, and they often are staffed mainly by volunteers and open for restricted hours, sometimes only two or three afternoons per week. But they have been growing rapidly during the past two or three decades; they are promising to become stronger and are meeting higher professional standards. In any case, even the weaker ones usually are saving valuable primary sources of material history.

## Collections of Curiosities

Most of the early museums were collections of curiosities[1] or oddments. In 1782 Pierre Eugène du Simitière (1736–1784) opened the American Museum in his Philadelphia home. Though it contained mainly library materials with which he hoped to write a history of the American Revolution, he did collect coins and medals, natural history specimens, Indian antiquities, and rarities. They included a Hession grenadier's cap with its brass ornament, and the shield, sword, and lance that his friend Captain John André used in the Meschianza tournament that honored Sir William Howe during the English army's occupation of Philadelphia. Du Simitière charged fifty cents to guide visitors about his holdings, but he died two years later before he could achieve his dream of establishing a national museum.

Charles Willson Peale (1741–1827) had the best of the early collections in his Philadelphia Museum, opened in 1786 and lasting under his sons until about 1850. The museum was devoted mainly to natural history and art but it contained American Indian objects as well as Oriental wares brought back by sea captains engaged in the China trade. Peale collected, conserved, and exhibited his holdings with much ingenuity; and though he believed in providing "rational amusement" (for example, live animals, a pipe organ, electrical machine, compound blowpipe for chemical experiments, physiognotrace, and Magic Mirrors) in order to attract numerous viewers at twenty-five cents a head, he did not resort to showing freaks or indulging in vaudeville acts. Curiosity or entertainment museums dominated the American scene for a time. Found in most good-sized towns, they were the property of individual entrepreneurs, "usually very unlearned persons," an English visitor reported, "who use them as sort of a provincial theatre" with "farces, songs, dances and similar entertainments," which form "the chief source of their revenue."[2]

The American Museum (1791) in New York is a good example of that kind of organization, running from the time of Gardiner Baker (died, 1798) through the period dominated by that astute showman, Phineas Taylor Barnum (1810–1891). The museum did little more in the historical area than show crude waxwork representations of American heroes from Washington to Andrew Jackson or present sensational exhibits such as a guillotine with its waxen beheaded victim and the French revolutionist Marat assassinated in his bath by Charlotte Corday. It gave major attention to using freaks, American Indians, vaudeville skits, and moral dramas to attract heavy visitation.

By about 1870 the more serious museums, including those devoted to history, had won out over their curiosity, entertainment rivals. They were governed, not by a single individual for his own profit, but by a board, the members of which usually came to be called trustees. Those museums did not depend entirely (in fact, in some cases not at all) upon admission fees for their income.

## Independent Historical Societies

The three earliest American historical societies[3] are the Massachusetts Historical Society (1791), New-York Historical Society (1804), and American Antiquarian Society (1812). John Pintard (1759-1844), a New York merchant whom a friend described as "a lively cheerful man, who appears . . . not to want understanding as much as he does solidity," and as "a singular mixture of heterogeneous particles,"[4] has been called "the Father of historical societies."[5] He dreamed of founding an organization similar to the Society of Antiquarians of London. He communicated his idea to the Reverend Jeremy Belknap (1744–1798) of Boston, author of an esteemed history of New Hampshire, who then formed the Massachusetts Historical Society. In addition to a library, its collection was to include "observations and descriptions in natural history and topography, together with specimens of natural and artificial curiosities, and a selection of every thing that can improve and promote the historical knowledge of our country, either in a physical or political view."[6] Julian Boyd was right in deeming that statement "a charter of the historical society movement."[7] Belknap was a true activist collector; he stated that "There is nothing like having a *good repository,* and keeping a *good-lookout,* not waiting at home for things to fall into the lap, but prowling about like a wolf for the prey."[8]

Pintard managed to persuade the St. Tammany's Society to establish the American Museum in New York but was disappointed to see it deteriorate into a collection of curiosities and oddments. He tried again and succeeded in setting up the New-York Historical Society, "the object of which," according to its constitution, was "to collect and preserve whatever may relate to the natural, civil, literary, and ecclesiastical History of the United States in general and of this State in particular."[9] It was encouraged "by the honorable example of the Massachusetts Society" and had a responsible board with Pintard as recording secretary. The breadth of its interests was shown when it appointed committees to collect zoology, botany, and vegetable physiology; mineralogy and fossils; coins and medals; manuscripts and books. The society treated Pintard somewhat shabbily. He agreed to sell it his library at cost; he could not afford to make it as a gift for he unwisely had signed some of his friends' notes, which landed him in debtor's prison for a time. The society still owed him $1,400 on the library account in 1827, a debt which it avoided paying.

Isaiah Thomas (1749–1831), distinguished pioneer newspaper publisher, collector, and historian of printing, organized the American Antiquarian Society in Worcester, Massachusetts. Thomas said that the chief objects of the society's collection were to be "American antiquities, natural, artificial, and literary; not, however, excluding those of other countries" and "specimens, with written accounts respecting them, of fossils, handicrafts or Aborigines, &c."[10]

All the first three societies had much broader objectives than we should assign to a historical society today, and they later narrowed their scope so as better to serve the political and cultural history of their regions. The Massachusetts Society gave up its natural curiosities to the Boston Society of Natural History (1830) and the Peabody Museum (1866) at Harvard and lent its good silver collection to the Museum of Fine Arts. Though it retained valuable portraits and a few historical objects that included Benjamin Franklin's matrices of type, a gorget and epaulets of George Washington, and the pen with which Lincoln signed the Emancipation Proclamation, the society did not maintain a museum but used its holdings for decoration of its headquarters and for special exhibitions. It devoted itself wholly to historical scholarship with outstanding library, manuscripts, and publications.

The Antiquarian Society for a time had a distinguished anthropological collection with American Indian materials including archaeological specimens from Midwestern mounds, and Central and South American pre-Columbian objects. The first librarian, Christopher Columbus Baldwin, however, thought it "absurd to pile up old bureaus and chests, and stuff them with old coats and hats and high-heeled shoes," and his successor, Samuel Foster Haven, declared that the society was "intended for scientific use and gratification of enlightened curiosity" and was not "a mere museum of articles for idle and unprofitable inspection."[11]

Beginning in 1886 its archaeological and ethnological collections went to the Peabody Museum at Harvard, and in 1908 Librarian Clarence S. Brigham sent various objects to the Worcester Art Museum, Worcester Historical Society, and Smithsonian Institution. Museum functions were discontinued unless they had some historical association with its books or manuscripts. The society definitely considered itself a research library and made every effort to accumulate superb imprints, manuscripts, and newspapers. Both the Massachusetts and the Antiquarian societies were unusual in that they restricted their membership to a certain number of elected scholars.

The New-York Historical Society, though it did dispose of its natural history collection in 1829 to the Lyceum of Natural History, accepted Plains Indian and pre-Columbian artifacts from Central and South America, American and European paintings of the New York Gallery of Fine Arts (that contained Luman Reed's Collection), thirteen huge marble bas-reliefs from Nineveh, Dr. Henry Abbott's Egyptian Collection, the best in the country with three spectacular mummified bulls, and the 433 mainly European canvases of Thomas Jefferson Bryan's Gallery of Christian Art. In 1868 the society, then the city's premier art collection, tried to raise funds to organize its varied holdings as a great museum of history, antiquities, and art. The state of New York gave it a tract of land in Central Park between 81st and 84th streets, but when the society campaign for funds failed, transferred the land to the newly founded Metropolitan Museum of Art. The society later lent the Egyptian Collection, Nineveh marbles, and Plains and pre-Columbian materials to the Brooklyn Museum, which ultimately purchased most of them. A court decision allowed it to exchange or sell its European paintings. The society continues today as a leading research library, but also as a first-rate museum of New York cultural materials which it uses in a strong program of exhibitions and educational activities for both adults and schoolchildren.

By the time of the Centennial Exposition at Philadelphia in 1876, there were seventy American historical societies, most of them situated in every state east of Texas. The independent, privately organized societies were by far the most numerous. In the main they followed the models of the Boston and Antiquarian societies in that they sought to attract scholars (though not through restricted membership) who would help build their research libraries and use them to produce historical articles and books, many of which the societies would publish. The Historical Society of Pennsylvania (1824) in Philadelphia was a good example of that kind of society, and its cautious attitude toward museum objects was shown by one of its early officers who promised to resist its becoming a "receptacle of antique trash."[12]

Yet, through the years many independent societies acquired historic houses, often as their headquarters, and began to build decorative art collections in order to furnish them, while others were persuaded to form museums by accepting collections of objects as gifts. The state societies of all the New England states, except Massachusetts, ended up with numerous museum collections. The Virginia Historical Society (1831) at Richmond began as a conservative, scholarly organization but made concessions to the museum function when, in 1946, it took over Battle Abbey, with Confederate battle flags, military portraits, and Civil War weapons and, in 1949, began to operate the endowed, magnificent Virginia House, built from remnants of English mansions. Maryland (1844) at Baltimore acquired an art gallery with copies of European masterpieces but resolved that "the Gallery should be kept in its subordinate relations: that it should not swallow up the Historical Society."[13]

Not all the independent societies were statewide in scope. The Essex Institute (1848) at Salem, Massachusetts was the oldest county historical society in the nation, with an excellent library and museum, as well as several historic house properties after 1910. The Chicago Historical Society (1856) is one of the strongest historical societies in the country, with a growing regional library and extensive museum. The New Haven Colony Historical Society (1862) in Connecticut secured a worthwhile collection of fine and decorative arts, and the Pocumtuc Valley Memorial Association (1870) played an important part in the preservation, restoration, and furnishing of eighteenth- and nineteenth-century houses in Deerfield, Massachusetts.

## State-Supported Historical Societies

Wisconsin formed a private state historical society[14] in 1846, two years before reaching statehood. For a time some wished to restrict membership as the Massachusetts and American Antiquarian societies had done, but the arrival in Madison of Lyman Copeland Draper (1815–1891), the driving collector of manuscripts, books, and other materials of the trans-Allegheny frontier, changed all that. Under the charter of the State Historical Society of Wisconsin of 1854, it was open to everyone who paid dues of a dollar a year, and Draper, always the skilled promoter, as corresponding secretary, used numerous honorary memberships and exchanges with other societies to build an important research library, portrait gallery, and small cabinet of museum objects. The state legislature in 1854 granted the society $500 with which to purchase library materials and, the next year, doubled that amount, with $500 for Draper's salary. Wisconsin was the first state to make regular annual appropriations for its historical society and has continued that practice ever since.

Draper's chief museum activity was building a portrait gallery. He sent many American artists handsomely engraved certificates making them honorary members and requesting examples of their work. He induced governors and other political, industrial, and cultural leaders to present their likenesses and managed to finance portraits of important Indian chiefs. In 1886 the gallery contained 135 paintings, mainly portraits but some representations of Wisconsin towns, canals, and battlefields of the Black Hawk War. They constituted a documentary view of the early state and were useful in securing legislative support from the leaders whose portraits graced the gallery. Other museum materials included coins, medals, Indian antiquities (especially the Perkins Collection of rare copper implements), objects of pioneer life, and Civil War military equipment.

Draper chose as his successor in 1887 Reuben Gold Thwaites (1853–1913), a Madison newspaper editor, who became the most successful historical society director that the nation had known. He saw clearly that a publicly supported historical society needed to serve the historical interests of the whole state, and he welcomed not only skilled research scholars and historical editors like himself, but also genealogists, local historians, public school students, in fact anyone seeking information on Wisconsin and American history. Thwaites considered the society's museum "the department of our work which chiefly appeals to the general public."[15] It attracted legislators, university faculty and students, visitors seeing the sights of the state capital, and numerous school classes.

Thwaites secured from the state a fine building on the University of Wisconsin campus, and the society's library with its valuable manuscripts and newspapers constituted the history section of the university's library holdings. The active program of public education and service paid off, not only in generous state appropriations, but also in support from the university, women's clubs, patriotic societies, schools, and individuals. The society began to preserve several historic houses situated about the state.

Among other Midwestern states that supported historical societies with public funds were Minnesota (1849) at St. Paul, later with dynamic directors Solon J. Buck and Theodore C. Blegen; Iowa (1857) at Iowa City; Kansas (1875) at Topeka; and Ohio (1885) at Columbus. All developed museums except Iowa, which had a separate Department of Archives and History (1892) with a museum in Des Moines. Ohio, Minnesota, and Kansas were especially successful in establishing historical museum branches, Ohio still with more than thirty of them. Ohio and Kansas more recently have placed their central museums on interstate highways, thus greatly increasing their attendance.

## State Historical Departments

Ten states have established departments of history as governmental branches.[16] A state historical society may accompany the department and sometimes hold meetings and issue some publications, but the department is in charge and customarily operates a library, central and branch museums, and a publishing program. Some of the strongest of these are situated in Alabama (1901) at Montgomery; Mississippi (1902) at Jackson with its Mississippi State Historical Museum; North Carolina (1903) at Raleigh with central museum and a score of historic houses; and the Pennsylvania Historical and Museum Commission (1945) at Harrisburg with a good museum there and fifty branch museums around the state.

## Historic House Museums

The historic house museum[17] consists of a carefully preserved or restored structure, often with outbuildings, original or period furnishings, and consonant landscape setting or garden. It may have been a residence, shop, manufactory, town hall, schoolhouse, or served some other purpose. The Jonathan Hasbrouck House (1725) on the Hudson River at Newburgh, New York, was the first such American museum in 1850. It had been General Washington's headquarters in the last year of the Revolution. Andrew J. Caldwell, a persistent lawyer serving as commissioner of the United States Deposit Fund, persuaded Governor Hamilton Fish to save the house; the governor had the New York legislature acquire the property and maintain and operate it with the Newburgh Village Trustees as custodians. They were "to keep it as it was during General Washington's occupancy."[18]

Of much greater influence, however, was Mount Vernon, Washington's plantation on the Potomac River below Washington, D.C. Attempts to have the federal government or the Commonwealth of Virginia acquire and operate the property failed, but Ann Pamela Cunningham (1816–1875) of South Carolina, a frail but determined maiden lady, began a successful campaign in 1853 to save the plantation as a shrine. She founded the Mount Vernon Ladies' Association of the Union with herself as regent and with viceregents from thirty-one states. She persuaded John Augustine Washington, Jr., great-grandnephew of Washington, to sell the 200-acre estate for $200,000 and with the help of the viceregents and their lady managers in counties and municipalities, raised the money. She enlisted Edward Everett, the silver-tongued senator from Massachusetts, to help; driven by the hope that admiration for Washington by both the North and South might avert the threatening sectional conflict, he gave an oration on the Father of His Country 129 times throughout the land as far west as St. Louis and raised $69,024 toward the purchase.

The Ladies' Association opened Mount Vernon in 1860. Miss Cunningham took a sound, common-sense attitude toward historic preservation; she wished "to preserve with sacred reverence" Washington's house and grounds "in the state he left them."[19] When declining health forced her to retire as regent in 1874, following her hero's example, she wrote a Farewell Address, which contained the stirring admonition:

> Ladies, the home of Washington is in your charge. See to it that you keep it the home of Washington! Let no irreverent hand change it; no vandal hands desecrate it with the fingers of *progress*. Those who go to the house in which he lived and died, wish to see in what he lived and died! Let one spot in this grand country of ours be saved from "change"! Upon you rests this duty.[20]

Miss Cunningham's success marked an important advance in women's rights in America. Her main organization of regents, viceregents, and lady managers was entirely female. Men were called upon when they could be useful—a lawyer to draw the charter; Senator Everett to raise money; George Washington Riggs, prominent Washington banker, to serve as treasurer; a small male advisory committee; and, of course, legislators to pass bills in Virginia and Congress. But Mount Vernon proved that imaginative and energetic women were abundantly able to plan an important and complex project, raise money for its purchase and operation, and run it effectively year after year.

Mount Vernon's impact on the historic house museum movement was great. It demonstrated the worth of a privately controlled, self-perpetuating cultural organization. It became the admired model of similar projects, such as Valley Forge and Stenton in Pennsylvania, the Hermitage in Tennessee, the William Henry Harrison House in Indiana, the George Walton House in Georgia, Abraham Lincoln's log-cabin birthplace in Kentucky, and in Virginia, Jefferson's Monticello, the Lees' Stratford, and George Mason's Gunston Hall. By 1895 there were some twenty historic house museums, but the coming of the automobile caused them to blossom in the countryside.

The next step forward for historic house museums came with the creation of a chain of them under a wise central administration. The pioneer of that movement was William Sumner Appleton (1874-1947) of Boston, who in 1910 founded the Society for the Preservation of New England Antiquities. Sumner Appleton was an imaginative enthusiast—smiling, patient, democratic, and modest. He was determined to preserve old buildings of historical importance or possessed of architectural and aesthetic quality. He used historical and architectural research to assure their authenticity, employed restoration only when absolutely necessary, and tried to keep structures on their original sites. For each building he sought a function that was financially feasible. Some of them, in favorable locations, could become house museums. Others might be sold or leased, under restrictions to guarantee their preservation, as residences or for adaptive uses as inns, offices, community centers, antique shops, tearooms, and the like. The Harrison Gray Otis House (1795) became the society's headquarters and central museum in Boston. In his thirty-seven years as corresponding secretary (or director), Appleton secured for the Society more than fifty houses throughout New England.

The Historic Sites Act of 1935 brought the federal government and the National Park Service into the history museum field when it declared it "a national policy to preserve for historic use historic sites, buildings, and objects of national significance for the inspiration and benefit of the people of the United States."[21] The Historic Preservation Act of 1966 established the National Register of Historic Places, made it difficult for federal agencies to harm registered landmarks, and soon began to provide matching grants for their maintenance. The National Trust for Historic Preservation, a private organization formed in 1949, operated a growing number of house museums of its own but chiefly advised and assisted its numerous member organizations and individuals.

The central bodies mentioned are directed at historic preservation in general, but they also foster and assist historic house museums. States and state historical societies play an increasing role in developing historic house branches. All this activity has meant that historic houses constitute the most numerous type of the American museum, numbering about two thousand today.

### Indoor Museums

The formation of an American national museum,[22] at first devoted mainly to natural history, began with the chartering of the Smithsonian Institution by Congress in 1846. James Smithson, the illegitimate son of an English duke, rather surprisingly had left his residuary estate worth more than $500,000 "to the United States of America, to found in Washington, under the name of the Smithsonian Institution, an establishment for the increase and diffusion of knowledge among men."[23] The 1846 act was a compromise that called for scientific research but also for a large building (still popularly known as the "Castle") to contain a museum, library, art gallery, chemical laboratory, and lecture room. The governing board of regents appointed as secretary (or director) Joseph Henry (1797–1878), one of the country's best scientists who specialized in the study of electromagnetism.

Henry thought "increasing of knowledge" or "enlarging the bounds of human thought by original research,"[24] by far the more important purpose of the bequest. He begrudged spending any of the slender annual income of $30,000 to $40,000 on a museum, library, art gallery, or lectures. He argued that the "diffusion of knowledge" requirement would be fulfilled by publishing new scientific work in the *Smithsonian Contributions to Knowledge* volumes and exchanging them with the publications of other scientific and learned societies throughout the country and the world. The Smithsonian was entitled to receive all museum objects that belonged to the federal government, and it opened the United States National Museum in 1858, taking over the "National Collection of Curiosities," until then displayed in the Patent Office Building. This occurred, however, only after Congress agreed to pay for new cases, moving expenses, and $4,000 yearly for maintenance.

In 1876 the Smithsonian sent exhibits to the Centennial Exhibition at Philadelphia, and when that world's fair closed, many states and thirty-four foreign governments donated to the Smithsonian materials of natural science, art, history, and technology that they had exhibited. The Castle and several nearby buildings were crammed with exhibits and storage, and Congress finally voted to finance a new structure (now the Arts and Industries Building), which opened in 1881. Henry's assistant secretary, Spencer Fullerton Baird (1823–1887), a leading naturalist, believed in museums that would both conduct research and enlighten the public. When he became secretary upon Henry's death, the National Museum began to thrive. Baird placed George Brown Goode (1851–1896) in charge of the museum, and he served also as curator of its department of arts and industries. Goode proved to be the most accomplished museum professional that had yet appeared in the country, and he skillfully developed the National Museum including its historical holdings. Today the Smithsonian's National Museum of American History (1964) is the largest and strongest indoor history museum in the nation.

Indoor museums made important contributions to the exhibition of historical material culture when they began to develop period rooms with authentic interior architecture and furnishings. The first ones in the country appeared at the Essex Institute in 1907 when its curator, George Francis Dow (1868–1936), installed a kitchen (1750), parlor (1800), and bedroom (1800) based on careful research, and then added one of Salem's oldest buildings, the John Ward House (1684, etc.), in the institute's backyard as a kind of miniature outdoor museum. Henry Watson Kent (1866–1948), the busy assistant secretary/curator of the Metropolitan Museum of Art, took the concept further when he organized a special loan exhibition of American paintings, furniture, silver, and other decorative art in observance of the Hudson-Fulton Celebration of 1909.

The first important show of American antiques, it attracted heavy and enthusiastic attendance. As a result, with Kent's avid promotion, the museum began to collect in those fields. In 1924 it opened its American Wing with a dozen eighteenth- and early nineteenth-century original rooms, all meticulously furnished. The American Wing had tremendous influence, not only on art museums such as the Philadelphia Museum of Art and the Museum of Fine Arts in Boston, but upon a host of historic houses and later upon Colonial Williamsburg in Virginia and the Henry Francis du Pont Winterthur Museum in Delaware.

Several cities have good indoor history museums. In addition to that of the Chicago Historical Society mentioned above, they include the Museum of the City of New York (1923), the Detroit Historical Museum (1928), and the Atwater Kent Museum (1939) in Philadelphia.

## Outdoor Museums

The outdoor museum[25] may be defined as a group of buildings that represents a historic village. The buildings are authentic themselves, usually with truthfully furnished interiors and appropriate landscape settings or gardens. In a sense the outdoor museum is an extension of the historic house museum concept. It is of two chief types: an actually preserved or restored town with original or restored buildings *in situ*, a considerable number of them authentically furnished and open to public visitation; or original buildings moved from their historic sites to a neutral spot so as to form a composite village, preferably one based on a sound historical conception. In either case the outdoor museum usually is interpreted by costumed "inhabitants," or "crafts persons," or "townspeople" who perform historic domestic or industrial tasks. Thus, the outdoor museum is said to present "living history." Though the preserved or restored town type of outdoor museum may partially resemble what today is called a historic district, many historic districts are not true outdoor museums. The historic districts, begun in the 1930s in Charleston and New Orleans, have expanded greatly under the Historic Preservation Act of 1966 and are found today in hundreds of cities. While the exteriors of their buildings are usually authentic, these buildings contain modern occupants, who simply enjoy the pleasant atmosphere of the external period surroundings and whose living arrangements and adaptive uses make no attempt to present history.

The first notable preservation/restoration kind of outdoor museum was Colonial Williamsburg, which in 1926 began to restore the eighteenth-century capital of Virginia. The Reverend Dr. W. A. R. Goodwin, an Episcopal rector, had the idea of using Williamsburg's eighty-five surviving original buildings as the basis for recreating a whole colonial village. He persuaded John D. Rockefeller, Jr., to share his dream and to finance and participate in the planning of the pioneering venture. Kenneth Chorley (1893–1974) served as the project's capable chief executive for some thirty years and managed to solve many of the problems that arose in a restoration that had never before been attempted on such a large scale. It strove to use historical, architectural, archaeological, and curatorial research to obtain truthful buildings, furnishings, settings, and interpretation. It employed carefully trained, costumed guides, an orientation center with an introductory historical film, dozens of craft demonstrations, special events such as carriage rides, militia drills, concerts, plays, and activities at Christmas and other holidays, and some interpreters who followed a first-person, dramatic approach in enacting historical roles.

An extensive publications program of books and audiovisual materials served not only local visitors but took the Williamsburg story throughout the country. The project allowed staff members as well as some overnight visitors to occupy some of its one hundred or so buildings situated on more than 175 acres. That approach brought the sights and sounds of ordinary living to the project each day. Colonial Williamsburg also operated hotels, restaurants (some using eighteenth-century recipes), and a decorative arts reproduction program, all of which served the visitors but also provided financial support for the historical activities.

The first large outdoor museum that moved buildings to a neutral spot was opened at Dearborn, Michigan, in 1929 by Henry Ford, the automobile manufacturer. He previously had established a historic house museum in 1923 at the Wayside Inn in Sudbury, Massachusetts, and Greenfield Village at Dearborn was part of a larger complex that included the Henry Ford Museum, which contained both historical and industrial/technology displays. Ford was an omnivorous collector who bought out whole antique shops and used his motor company dealers to obtain old buildings as well as power equipment and industrial objects.

Greenfield Village was laid out according to Ford's personal whim without a clearly defined purpose, and he refused to use professional museum personnel. It included birthplaces, craft shops, and laboratories connected with his own life and those of the Wright Brothers, his close friends Thomas Edison and Luther Burbank, and Charles Steinmetz. There were also a New England village green; Stephen Foster's birthplace; the sternwheeler steamboat *Suwanee*; the birthplace and schoolhouse of William Holmes McGuffey of the famed *Readers* as well as other schoolhouses, all of them used to educate young students of the neighborhood; and from England the stone Cotswold "Rose Cottage," with forge, dovecote, and stable, and the Sir John Bennett Jewelry Shop from Cheapside in London with its huge statues of Gog and Magog. The whole village contained more than one hundred structures and covered 260 acres.

A somewhat different example of that type of outdoor museum is found at Old Sturbridge Village in Massachusetts, which opened in 1946 on a 250-acre tract. It was started to display the extensive collection of antiquities, arts, and crafts made by two brothers, Albert B. and J. Cheney Wells, founders of the American Optical Company at Southbridge. Ruth (Mrs. George) Wells, Albert's daughter-in-law, was the first director of the village, and she was greatly aided by her husband. The village brought in typical original houses, shops, and other buildings from the New England region and soon decided to devote itself to showing New England life from 1790 to 1840, observing commendable historical accuracy. With costumed interpreters, working crafts persons, and a varied educational program that reached both adults and schoolchildren, it constituted a convincing living museum and attracted a large and appreciative audience.

Outdoor museums continue to spring up rapidly. Some of the leading ones are found at Mystic Seaport (1929) in Mystic, Connecticut; Farmers Museum (1942), Cooperstown, New York; Plimoth Plantation (1947), Plymouth, Massachusetts; Shelburne Museum (1947), Shelburne, Vermont; Old Salem (1950), Winston-Salem, North Carolina; Historic Deerfield (1951), Deerfield, Massachusetts; and Conner Prairie Pioneer Settlement (1964), Noblesville, Indiana. Most of them succeed in presenting a truthful picture of history based on intensive research, and their sound educational content is delivered in a lively but convincing manner that appeals to large audiences of all ages.

### Historical Museum Personnel

The persons connected with curiosity museums or with the historical societies that did not conduct museums obviously cannot be considered as early museum professionals.[26] Moreover, the staff administrators of the other organizations only slowly assumed the roles that the museum world considers proper today. Board members sometimes left their policy-making slots and took a hand in daily administration, a practice that is less prevalent now when most good museums allow the director (a term for the chief staff executive that has become common only in this century) to appoint and dismiss staff and conduct the everyday functions of collection, conservation, research, exhibition, and interpretation, subject, of course, to the policy setting and general supervision of the board.

Of the museum administrators mentioned in the preceding sections of this article, only Thwaites at the State Historical Society of Wisconsin, Buck and Blegen at Minnesota, Appleton of SPNEA, Dow of the Essex Institute (and later as Appleton's assistant), Baird and Goode at the Smithsonian, Kent of the Metropolitan Museum of Art, Ruth Wells of Old Sturbridge Village, and Chorley of Colonial Williamsburg may be considered genuine museum professionals. Only Buck, Blegen, Appleton, Baird, Goode, and Kent had formal education to prepare them for their posts, and that in subject matter (history, science, and library science). From that day up until recently, the better history museums were appointing directors who usually had obtained a degree (preferably graduate) in history or a related field, and their subject-matter knowledge was supplemented by the nuts and bolts museum techniques that they acquired on the job. Even then the museum administrative field remains so broad and varied that there is still room for a director with an entirely individualistic and unconventional background.

Museum studies courses that try to teach techniques and also require students to experience actual museum work in some kind of internship arrangement provide a relatively new kind of preparation. John Cotton Dana at the Newark (New Jersey) Museum in 1925 began to offer college graduates (usually young women) a year's apprenticeship in his innovative general museum that included historical objects. At about the same time, Professor Paul J. Sachs at Harvard and its Fogg Art Museum was teaching an excellent graduate course in museum work which, however, was concerned with art history. Today there are about a dozen well conceived and administered graduate courses available to prepare students for work in history museums.

Another valuable source of museum education is provided by several central museum organizations that furnish helpful annual meetings, publications, and special seminars that enable museum professionals to keep in touch with the latest developments in the field. Perhaps the three most useful of these are the American Association of Museums (with six related regional conferences), the American Association for State and Local History, and the International Council of Museums. The AAM has accreditation and museum assessment programs that help museums meet professional standards, and in 1984 it furnished future guidance with its publication, *Museums for a New Century.* The AASLH is engaged in a Common Agenda for History Museums program that is trying to improve standards for all history museums and especially the smaller ones. ICOM holds an international meeting every three years and has national committees in more than seventy-five countries around the world as well as twenty-two subject-matter committees that meet annually. Several other American organizations, including the

Smithsonian Institution, put on special seminars in museum techniques that are especially valuable for in-service training.

All of these recent developments prove that a museum profession is rapidly reaching maturity in America and that staff members are becoming aware of and actually meeting high professional standards in their work. History museums are actively participating in this professional advance.

# 1

# The Director's Mask

by

## Harold K. Skramstad, Jr.

HAROLD K. SKRAMSTAD, JR., is president of the Henry Ford Museum and Greenfield Village, Dearborn, Michigan. From 1974 to 1980 he was director of the Chicago Historical Society, prior to which time he served in several capacities on the staff of the National Museum of History and Technology of the Smithsonian Institution. He holds a Ph.D. in American civilization from George Washington University. Over the years Skramstad has been very active in historical preservation and in the museum field, serving as vice president of the American Association of Museums from 1984 to 1988 and as a member of the AAM Accreditation Commission and the Governmental Affairs Committee. He has published numerous articles and reviews pertaining to museums and has been a museum consultant in the areas of long-range planning, exhibits, and general management.

The "Suwanee," a steam-power stern wheeler that operates in Greenfield Village, was completely rebuilt by the museum's staff in 1989. Such projects show the wealth and diversity of skills represented by the staff. Courtesy of the Henry Ford Museum and Greenfield Village, Dearborn, Michigan.

*T*oday our society is much concerned about leadership. The innovative corporate CEO, for many years banished from public favor, has been restored to a position of popular hero in our culture. A flood of popular and academic literature focuses on the need for leadership in our society. This perceived need for leadership now fuels a multi-billion dollar industry of books, tapes, and seminars that offer all kinds of advice or plans or formulae for developing leadership in hopes of strengthening organizational performance. While it is easy to criticize much of this material, all indicators point to the fact that its existence is evidence of a general recognition that, in a rapidly changing and competitive world, the standards of performance of every organization must be raised, and that improving the quality of leadership is essential in raising those standards.

Certainly this is the case in historical organizations. Except for the very small, volunteer historical society that functions primarily as a community organization, historical organizations have had to reexamine both their position and performance in a new world of changed expectations. No longer is the genial and quiet scholar-administrator the role model for historical administrators any more than the antiquarian, slightly tattered, discouraged image of the historical society or historical museum is adequate as a model for today's historical organization.

If we agree that most of the prescriptions and formulas for leadership fail to address many of the complexities of people and organizations where then do we look for guidance?

*The Wizard of Oz* by Frank Baum is a delightful children's story, well told, that can help us understand some aspects of leadership that are too often missed by more adult literature. We all remember a climactic moment in the story when Dorothy and her companions pull away the curtain that surrounds the great Oz and find that behind this mask he is merely a *common man*. Yet too often we forget the larger lesson of Oz as leader: that any leader must be not only a shaper of vision and values but a reflector as well. So much attention is paid to defining the characteristics or qualities of leadership that what is forgotten is that leaders cannot be leaders without followers. It is the interaction between the leader of an organization and those others who have a stake in it that is key to any successful enterprize.

In defining the relationship between leaders and followers, the *director's mask* is an essential element. The mask functions not as a device to conceal, although it inevitably does conceal certain aspects of personality; instead it functions as a symbol of mutual strength and support that gains its power from both the director and the directed.

When followers look at the director's mask they must see what they both hope to see and are required to see. Their leader must be what they want and need to do their job. Although much of the public mask of Oz projects the personae of a tyrant and blowhard, there still exists a strong bond of affection between Oz and his followers. He demonstrates this quality in his recognition that he alone cannot legitimize his role as wizard. He cannot unilaterally give the lion courage, the scarecrow a brain, and the tin man a heart. These things can only be developed by them from within. The best thing Oz (or any director) can do is create a setting that allows others to do their best. The Wizard of Oz then functions primarily as a leader who allows others to perform better than they could without him. What he provides is the essential mask that projects his own sense of vision and purpose, and yet offers others with whom he comes in contact an opportunity to help shape the mask in a way that is meaningful and helpful to them.

The situation of the historical organization is not so different. No matter how established or mature the organization, it still functions primarily through purpose and people, and an interaction between the two. The director must hire the best people possible to move the organization ahead. This means he must find able people, professionally trained people, and knowledgeable people, with independent minds and strong personalities—the kind of people who will question and debate much of what the director wants to do, just the kind of people who want to go their own way.

The only way to keep this potentially unruly group on track is the necessary subordination of individual choices to institutional goals. Here the director's role is crucial. It is the director who must formally take on the role as official shaper and communicator of the organization's vision of what it fundamentally is and where it is going. The director's vision must be large enough to incorporate and respect the vision of others in order to command respect and loyalty. Once formed, this vision provides a gyroscope not only to guide but sustain the organization and those who have a stake in it. It must be always visible and understandable so that it answers many questions before they are asked. It is essential that the people who have a stake in the organization read and understand the director's mask the same way; if they read it differently or if its outline is unclear, it becomes difficult if not impossible for people to do their best work. They become instead overly cautious or unsure or unwilling to act.

There is a faulty assumption by many that the institutional vision falls like divine inspiration into the director's mind. The reality is that the organization's vision is created only by constant interaction with others whether they be members of the governing board, colleagues, staff, or members of the community. Goals, purpose, and even mission must constantly be reviewed, rethought, critically examined, reshaped, and updated. Just as the vision is becoming clear, just as it is being effectively communicated, parts of it inevitably are changing, being modified, or amended to adjust to new realities. Thus the director's basic responsibility for clarity of goal and purpose is inevitably flawed since by definition the continual process of organizational change means that there will always be a high degree of ambiguity and the unknown that must coexist with a clear sense of purpose.

Again, the crucial element is the bond of communication and respect between the director and others, especially staff, who have a stake in the organization. The director's mask provides the point where a clear and understandable organizational vision—a reliable and visible guide to thought and action—meets the somewhat hazy, out of focus, ambiguous world of change. Like the Wizard of Oz, the director must develop a mask that gives clear purpose and direction, yet which creates a bond of kinship with those upon whom he depends for success in everything the organization does.

There is little in the traditional background or development of historians to help the director develop the mask needed to lead a historical organization. Much of the historical and other professional training that forms the basic preparation for the historian's job is a barrier to effective leadership. Most historians have been trained in the basic issues underlying the pursuit of historical knowledge and in the use of the tools of historical research. The objective of the training is to develop a critical and independent mind whose primary loyalty is to a set of professional goals shared among other historians. In approaching the leadership of a historical organization, it is necessary to learn a new set of values and yet not forget the professional preparation that must necessarily provide an intellectual core of values for any director.

The shift from the creation of a professional mask to an institutional one requires a new learning style that is strategic or action oriented. In an institutional setting the outcome of strategic learning must be decisions, and decisions result in action. This is extremely frustrating to the historian whose research methods involve careful examination of sources, critical evaluations, and finally historical synthesis. In an institutional setting the learning and research style is quite different. There is never the leisure to think great thoughts, make great plans, and carry out extensive research prior to making a decision. The institutional agenda and the press of events outside the control of the organization inevitably conspire to prevent the systematic and more leisurely learning process of the historian. Yet in shaping the director's mask it is essential that the mask not lose the power of historical vision. The core value of any historical organization must be to *do* history. If the director's mask does not clearly incorporate historical values into its visible outline, it will lose much of its power to bond together leader and follower.

The shift from professional advocate to institutional leader also means that inevitably the visible role of the director becomes primarily that of an enabler. The director's mask must be seen by all as a visible and positive symbol for the organization. If its visage is always stern and critical, it will discourage rather than encourage. Yet at the same time the director cannot be seduced by his own cheer-leading. Like Oz, the director must recognize that the common man behind the mask has a responsibility to examine and reexamine continually and critically the assumptions behind the cheers. This constant critique will result in course corrections that then must be incorporated as a part of the mask, not so quickly that it creates confusion or so slowly it is unnoticed and thereby of no help in providing guidance.

Another important element in creating a successful director's mask is acceptance of responsibility for the work of others and the teaching and mentoring that go with that responsibility. The director is in a unique position within the organization to gather, sift, and redistribute information and insight. Perhaps more of the influence of the director is derived from this role than any other. Using information to provide vital linkages between people in the organization and the community is an important tool of empowerment that must be used constantly and positively. If it is used instead as a method of control to reward or punish, the power of the mask diminishes and the bond of trust that the mask creates and sustains is made weaker.

The role of the director in any organization is a complex one as many of the essays in this volume point out. Yet at the root of all the many roles, the job description of the director is quite simple. It is the director's responsibility to be the communicator of the organization's vision and the custodian of the organization's values. These two responsibilities underlie everything else the director does. To carry out these two responsibilities is not easy. To communicate both internally and externally the vision of what an organization stands for and where it is going requires a willingness to share in the process of shaping that vision. To be custodian of the values of an organization requires setting and holding to high standards of performance and personal integrity for everyone.

The director's mask, then, is a key element in providing a clear image of the director as institutional representative, but it must not be so overpowering as to discourage its use as a mirror for constant testing and growth by others in the organization. If the mask is successfully wrought, it can have great power for good in the organization. Just as the Wizard of Oz could help the lion discover his own courage, the scarecrow his brain, and the tin man his heart, the director can enable the people in the organization to develop and nurture the reservoirs of courage, intelligence, and heart that exist in all of them.

# 2

# The Director as Intellectual Leader and Educator

by

Ellsworth H. Brown

ELLSWORTH H. BROWN has been president and director of the Chicago Historical Society since 1981. From 1976 to 1981 he was director of the Tennessee State Museum in Nashville. He began his career in museum work in 1971 as director of the Dacotah Prairie Museum in Aberdeen, South Dakota. He received his Ph.D. in American history from Michigan State University, his M.A. in the same field from Western Michigan University, and a B.A. from Hillsdale College (Michigan) in American history/English. Brown has taught at Vanderbilt University, the University of Tennessee at Nashville, and other institutions. Over the years he has been extremely active in professional affairs, principally with AASLH and the American Association of Museums. Currently he is the president of AAM.

Scholarly collaboration with the Chicago Historical Society on *A House Divided: America in the Age of Lincoln,* an exhibition that opened 28 January 1990. Left to right: Leon Litwack, Professor of History, University of California at Berkeley; Barbara Fields, Professor of History, Columbia University; Eric Foner, DeWitt Clinton Professor of History, Columbia University. Courtesy of the Chicago Historical Society, Chicago, Illinois.

*T*he director in these collected essays has a golden future. Reality is a leveler, however, and trustees seeking a director must inevitably assess required strengths and permissible weaknesses. This essay argues that whatever else a director brings to the job, he or she must be an institution's intellectual leader. Security can be hired, legal advice may be secured otherwise, and donors contribute most readily when solicited by their peers. But the absence of intellectual and educational leadership creates a void that cannot be filled by anyone but a director. The staff's laissez-faire attempts to do so can be anarchic. The role is uncomfortable and inappropriate for anyone other than the director; a director must provide this leadership, or the institution will do without.

There are two chief questions to be considered: How does one become or be an intellectual leader? And where *should* one lead an institution? The second query is more significant, for if it is answered, the solution to the first question becomes somewhat obvious. Therefore, this essay is mostly about the second question and concludes with a consideration of the practical aspects that guide one in the deliberate execution of intellectual and educational leadership.

To be measured, leadership must be compared to a benchmark, the most common of which is the status quo. But the status quo is not only the state of museums in 1990. It is also the state of history teaching, learning, and writing throughout the United States, in public schools as well as museums, and in colleges and universities. In other words the question of leadership—at least as far as this essay is concerned—must exist within the broad context of the academy and the community. A museum cannot measure itself, its leaders cannot be tested, and its mission cannot be fulfilled outside the framework of the public and its schools, academe, and the museum field.

It is clear that in some broad, diffused, and unplanned way the humanities have become part of the American fabric. Lynne V. Cheney, chairman of the National Endowment for the Humanities, offered one of the most optimistic views of this position in her short report *Humanities in America* (1988). "The remarkable blossoming of the humanities in the public sphere," she wrote, "is one of the least noted, though most important, cultural developments of the last few decades." A day's service on an endowment panel provides convincing testimony of the originality and diversity of humanities projects, including those of museums. In case one has missed such service, Cheney provides her own catalog of events large and small, in cities large and towns small, throughout the nation. Different explanations are offered for this phenomenon: a better educated public, a more mature nation, emergence from a cynical time. This happy if tempered view is not universally held—probably a matter of personal optimism or pessimism—but there is evidence to support it, and it confirms what most of us in museums would like to think.

What intellectual challenge can the museum director find in this fermenting interest in the humanities? One can seek the degree to which interest has progressed in a given community, in what niches it can be found and nurtured, and in what way one's museum can contribute to and capitalize on the new order. It may be necessary to show a community the way. In some cases it may be enough to show a museum the direction in which a community has already traveled. The important point is that the museum director must be consciously aware of the trend and make an equally conscious effort to assess whether compatible initiatives are possible or desired. Intuition or a vague sense of movement is not sufficient, however.

If the public acquits itself well in the measure of the humanities, America's schools do not—at least according to Merrill D. Peterson, who wrote an affirming and prescriptive piece called *The Humanities and the American People* on behalf of the Colloquium on the Humanities and the American People. From Peterson's piece one can discern by inference the shortcomings of humanities in the broad sweep of American life and especially the stark inadequacies of public school systems. Peterson would appear to be one whose view is not optimistic, but he provides a wonderfully affirmative and prescriptive discussion of how the humanities can be advanced.

Other assessments confirm the desperate state of public education. Cheney's first report, *American Memory* (1987), addressed schools' plight in the humanities. An exceptionally focused article by Paul Gagnon called "Why Study History?"[1] cuts to the quick in its analysis of public school history education, which is too little taught to promote civic judgment.

More disturbing than the state of the humanities in the schools is the state of teaching of any kind, especially in the public schools of large cities. The scale of the problem renders the importance of a discussion about the teaching of history itself insignificant, as the *Chicago Tribune's* investigative series "Chicago Schools: Worst in America" makes graphically clear. Indeed, one of the Chicago Historical Society's educators, providing in-school services, reported that reality in the schools was appreciably worse than the *Tribune's* series suggested.

Whether *the director as educator* refers to one's role vis à vis staff or as a leader in the education of a museum's constituents, the challenge has the potential to be all-consuming.

What is the status quo in the field of academic history? This is difficult to assess, but Gagnon argues that the field is much taken with details but less committed to providing synthesis, the large view, the sweep of history, and the conclusions that make the details useful. This generalization may be more applicable to new disciplines such as urban history, which will be fifty in 1990, but papers delivered to the Chicago Historical Society's Urban History Seminar tend to confirm such an opinion. A survey of *Reviews in American History* partially confirms it too; and Cheney, in *Humanities in America*, contends that "As specialization becomes ever narrower, the humanities tend to lose their centrality. The large matters they address can disappear in a welter of detail."

If the field of history is thus handicapped, the challenge to the museum director of sorting out the important details and locating the synthesis that makes history useful and instructive is more demanding than it ought to be. Fortunately, there is hope. Whatever the condition of history as a field, it is clear that the linkages between scholars in the academic community and scholars in museums are new and strengthening. The National Endowment for the Humanities has long required the joining of scholars from both the academic and museum communities, and the endowment remains one of the leading and primary forces in this cause. Lately the Common Agenda for History Museums, cosponsored by the American Association for State and Local History and the Smithsonian Institution, has urged the seeking of a common agenda for academic and museum scholars. Professional historical journals have recently begun to review exhibitions, driven by a conscious effort to include museums and by the beginning reciprocity of these institutions. And the now forming American Urban History Association is considering, from its outset, the inclusion of museum exhibitions among the subjects eligible for awards.

The foregoing is not an apology for museums and does not suggest that museums are complete until they have linked with academic scholars. Museums are humanities institutions. They need no linkage with "bona fide" scholars in colleges and universities to confirm their worth and legitimacy. But the measure of a director's intellectual leadership must include the degree to which the institution broadens the rings of the circle and contributes to a more holistic humanities network.

And what of the museums throughout the nation? The larger ones can indeed afford a rich array of intellectual stimulae. Their directors, aided by larger and more specialized staff and better travel budgets, may not need the advice of this piece. They hire advisors—historians, sociologists, some borrowed from academe, and some hired as permanent staff. Lynne Cheney says as much, for the stellar museum programs that she cites are chiefly from large institutions: the Los Angeles Museum of Natural History, the New York Public Library, the Walters Art Gallery, the Art Institute of Chicago. One exemplar humanities exhibition, the recent "William Wordsworth and the Age of English Romanticism," had a rental fee of $150,000, plus installation and promotion costs. The power of the larger organizations to effect increased awareness of history is wonderful.

On the other hand, the traveler who frequents smaller, usually local museums has long been able to describe stereotypical installations. Whatever the uniqueness of the community, there is usually a strong dose of pioneer history and numbers of spinning wheels, wedding dresses, Victorian parlors, perhaps a kitchen (always popular, "a good teaching tool"), and an assortment of photographs, books, scrapbooks, and miscellaneous serials that are duplicated at the public library. Many have far to go before they deal with important (genuinely local) history.

This returns us to our earliest questions. How does one become or be an intellectual leader? And where *should* one lead an institution? The director must fasten upon some operating premises. And the first of these ought to be that humanists must have the gentle arrogance not only to ask questions—the classic "We only raise questions; it is up to the viewer to provide the answer"—but also *answer* questions. If we believe that the humanities provide a way to greater civic judgment, or greater personal happiness or understanding or even contentiousness, we ought to be bold enough to seek and advance answers to problems.

The second premise might be that museums ought to deal with large questions of history or synthesized history. This does not omit local history or local museums; it is not about size of exhibitions. Rather, it is about the kinds of questions and answers that are used: Why was the community built? Would we build it again if we started today? What has changed? How has the community adjusted? Why are there (or aren't there) minorities in the community? How has migration of Jews in America changed them; why did migration of Scandinavian groups to America freeze their culture in stereotypical ways? Why was the progressive movement active in Wisconsin and not so active in Tennessee?

Third, the museum ought to engage the community on its own terms. If the town is small and the school system good, small and easily accessible enrichment programs might be sufficient. If the city is Chicago, perhaps a museum ought to seek funds to hire buses and bring school children to the institution or place a teacher in the schools or adopt several inner-city schools and provide special help—all of these things have been done. Engagement is much easier to accept and much more challenging to effect if the first two premises are accepted. The museum director is an intellectual leader if he or she subscribes to such assumptions, holds these or other clearly defined ideas up for examination, and articulates them as part of the mission of the institution.

There are certain tools or means of action available to the director, who ought to deliberately preserve the flexibility of the role, the ability to roam through various communities—legal, aesthetic, intellectual, guardian, and public. This is the wonderful gift of a directorship, and it must be protected from the encroachment of daily demands. To some extent the job itself provides the necessary avenues, but the contacts must be nurtured and returned to. Circulation, networks, travel, and reading are complementary ways of preserving this role.

Need the director be an intellectual? Or an educator? Is practicality sufficient? The answer is yes, any of these. The director can be any one of several kinds of people, as long as he or she is aware of the tools that are available. Consider linkages with academe, for example. They can be local, forged over lunch; they can be national—a carefully planned bi-annual trip to a state, regional, or professional historical conference should raise questions and provide names of historians thinking sufficiently that the astute director can establish a bank of resources and ideas.

The single most important tool of the director, however, is the use of the simple question, coupled with untempered curiosity. The most powerful impressions of individuals that this writer carries are those formed by people who asked questions incessantly. The question—applied to contacts, used at conferences, asked in innocence or out of sophistication, asked as part of a concerted gathering of ideas and answers—is enabling even in fields beyond the director's immediate knowledge. It is enabling in the face of particular rather than synthesized history. And it is enabling when one helps others to discover answers. Questions, applied at the historical conference or museum meeting, are helpful. Questions that are applied to the work within a museum are critical. The intellectual leader of a museum asks questions even when the answers might be known and asks provocative questions and repetitive questions to test others' depth of analysis and the institution's investment in an idea. The leader forms committees and asks questions at meetings, charging the groups with finding answers and begging the questions with the premises discussed above.

This is a role that only a director can play, because it is a provocative and sometimes irritating role that requires the insulation a director enjoys. Open forums of discussion ought to exist in any organization, most of all in a humanistic institution. But the director must establish the framework and ask the most difficult questions. The director must be, by force of idea or process or query, the intellectual spine of a museum.

# 3

# The Social Responsibilities of History Museum Directors

by

## Robert R. Macdonald

ROBERT R. MACDONALD was appointed director of the Museum of the City of New York in 1985, prior to which he served as director of the Louisiana State Museum, executive director of the New Haven Colony Historical Society (Connecticut), and director/curator of the Mercer Museum of the Bucks County Historical Society (Pennsylvania). He holds a B.A. in history and an M.A. in American civilization from the University of Notre Dame and an M.A. in American civilization from the University of Pennsylvania. Mr. Macdonald has served in numerous museum leadership capacities, most notably as president of the American Association of Museums from 1985 to 1988, as vice president and secretary from 1982 to 1985, and as a member of both the AAM and AASLH councils. He has been active in exhibition development and in the editing of related publications during his museum career.

Former Mayor Edward I. Koch (left) of New York City and Director Robert Macdonald (right) of the Museum of the City of New York at the opening of the exhibition, *On Being Homeless: An Historical Perspective*, which was installed at the museum from 24 November 1987 to 27 March 1988. Courtesy of the Museum of the City of New York, New York, New York.

*H*istory museums comprise about half of all museums in the United States.[1] What small town is without a historic house? What metropolitan area does not claim a historical society or museum? Yet when Americans think of museums, the art, natural history, science or technology museum first comes to mind. When it is a question of public and private support and attention, history museums are among the weakest museums in the country. If most history museums are not viewed as vital community resources worthy of notice and commitment, it may be because history museum directors have failed to appreciate the traditional role of history and the responsibilities of history museum professionals and their institutions to society.

When considering the social responsibilities of museum directors, the public and the museum professional often confuse a director's obligations to attend cocktail parties and black-tie dinners with his or her responsibility to serve the public. Museum directors, particularly those of history museums, need to do more than keep their formal attire pressed or jewelry cleaned. The fundamental social responsibility of history museum directors is to focus the human, collection, and financial resources of their institutions on the transmission of historical information that is of meaningful educational benefit to their audiences.

Too few history museum directors in the United States have an understanding or appreciation of this responsibility. While knowledge of the past and the transmission of historical information have been constant and vital elements in all human societies, the directors of America's history museums have tended to view their role as passive collectors, preservers, and interpreters of history. They have valued the activities of their institutions as ends in themselves, disconnected from the needs or concerns of the consumers of the history being conserved and presented. Too little thought has been given to the relationship between historical interpretation and the impact of that interpretation on society. There appears to be a fear that the purposeful interpretation of history by museums as a means of educating the public is unscholarly, propagandistic, and perhaps even un-American. Critics of that concept view unfavorably the way the history museums of the Soviet Union and the People's Republic of China play a conscious role in transmitting knowledge and values. History museum directors in the United States prefer to believe that interpretation should be neutral, founded on scholarship, with the only message being that history is sufficient unto itself and need not relate to the needs of contemporary society. As a consequence America's history museums have become oases of nostalgia where ideas are rare and no one, least of all the visitor, is challenged. Believing that the only measure of their work should be methodology, many directors have opted to become "Dr. Feelgoods" and, to a large extent, have abandoned their responsibilities as historians and educators dedicated to the welfare of the communities their museums exist to serve.

The last authoritative analysis of American museums, *Museums U.S.A.: A Survey Report*, published by the National Endowment for the Arts in 1974, supports this characterization of historical museum directors. The survey asked museum directors from all types of museums to rate the purposes and functions of their institutions. In its summary the *Report* noted that, history museums differed sharply from museums of other classifications in the ranking of the importance of purposes. History museums indicated that 93 percent considered "conserving the cultural and/or scientific heritage" and "interpreting the past or present to the public" as very important. These proportions were substantially higher than for art and science museums. The directors of nonhistory museums, however, saw "providing educational experiences for the public" as the most important function of their institutions. While all museum directors surveyed viewed "encouraging positive social change" as of secondary importance, only 6 percent of historical museum directors saw this function as very important for their museums.[2]

The survey indicates that history museum directors do not view the interpretation of history as primarily an educational function or as an important means of promoting social change. If this inference is accurate, and the exhibitions and programs of the vast majority of the nation's history museums seem to confirm it, then one could conclude that today's history museum directors have a limited understanding of the social role of history or of their own professional responsibilities as historians and educators.

From the beginning of recorded history, knowledge and appreciation of the past have been central intellectual and emotional forces promoting the welfare of human societies. Knowledge of history has allowed individuals and communities to strengthen an understanding of place, time, and a civilizing sense of self. "Who am I?" and "Who are we?" are the central questions that history attempts to answer. In searching for the answers to these questions, mankind has produced the glue that binds human societies. Only a part of that glue is found in written history. Historically, human beings have sought answers to their individual and shared identity through oral traditions, music, visual and applied art and architecture, and other material documents of the past.

Although the world is a much more literate place today, man continues to seek individual and social consciousness through the history experienced rather than the history read. Comparatively few Americans study history and most view history as a dry, uninteresting subject of little practical value. Yet millions visit historical museums and sites, view historically based films, listen to traditional music, and talk history with their grandparents and other elderly authorities on the past.

The most important history for each of us is our own personal history. If few of us write biographies, nearly everyone curates his or her own historical collections. These *museums of self* are found hanging on the walls of homes and locked away in drawers or in trunks stored in the corner of the attic. Here are the portraits of ancestors, creased photographs from the Junior Prom, a ballet or Little League trophy, the ticket stubs to a favorite play, a letter from Mom. A visit to these personal collections renews a sense of self and well-being.

History museums are museums of self writ large containing the material evidence of a community's past. The community may be defined by geography, interest, time, activity or some other category. These *museums of community* can be found in the small rooms of village libraries or in major institutions employing hundreds and hosting thousands. They all share a common responsibility, within the parameters of their mission and resources, to collect, preserve, and present a history that has meaning and usefulness to their audiences. The subject of these museums may be the past, but in a democratic society they exist to meet the history needs of the present.

The relationship of history museum collections to contemporary needs and concerns poses a complex challenge for directors. It may not be immediately clear how collections inherited from the acquisitive activities of an earlier period can be readily interpreted to speak to the present. However, because the contemporary world is a continuum of the past, the values, information, techniques, and issues reflected in these holdings provide a dimension in which to address present-day concerns. The first step in meeting the challenge is for directors to view the collections they have inherited in new ways and to refocus their interpretation in light of what is perceived as important to their audiences. This requires that history museum directors be as sensitive to the world around them as they are knowledgeable about the past.

Just as no individual can save all the material documents of his or her life, so no historical museum can preserve and present the scope and depth of material culture that fulfills the institution's mission and meets the needs of its audiences. Mankind has always saved, preserved, and explored the objects of history that were viewed as having the most meaning at the moment. These were the materials that communities believed filled the need for historical understanding. Human societies ignored and disposed of materials that they viewed as having little value in meeting historical needs at any particular time. In the American experience the primary history need was seen as strengthening a sense of nationhood. Americans have used history to answer the questions of

"What is the United States?" and "Who are Americans?" They have had little difficulty in answering the first of these questions. But addressing who we are as a people has proved difficult.

Because most of the United States' early written history, collecting, and interpretive efforts were guided by descendants of Anglo-Saxon forefathers, the early America that was defined and memorialized was Anglo-Saxon in character. As a result today's history museums are filled with the material culture of this particular group. When collecting the physical evidence of other Americans, museums usually categorized and presented it as "folk"—somewhat out of the American mainstream. The history being presented was factual because it was based on authentic materials and was the history America thought it needed. This particular self-image was plucked from a vast pool of information and material culture that was no less authentic, just less relevant to a perceived need. In the process historical museums ignored and lost important evidence of a variety of other American people, experiences, and traditions.

Americans who grew up in the 1940s and 1950s spending Saturday afternoons at the cinema for twenty-five cents watching "Flash Gordon" serials will remember Emperor Ming of Mars, the paragon of evil with dark eyebrows and a spiked goatee. I have sometimes mused, *what if Ming sent an explorer to the United States and that explorer had time to visit only our historical museums? What would the people of Mars think of us?* The explorer's report would probably read, "Based on my first-hand observations of the materials found in the institutions established to preserve and present the history of these people, Americans are for the most part white, British, and Protestant. They are exceedingly wealthy, live in large mansions, wear fine clothes, and drink from silver cups. It appears that they have a habit of going to war with their enemies, but there is little evidence of conflict or controversy among themselves."

The Martian's analysis would be accurate, because it would have been based on the available historical evidence. But would Ming and the people of Mars have a clear understanding of the development of the United States as it approaches the end of the twentieth century? More to the point, have historical museums collected and presented a history that is useful in furthering an understanding of ourselves and our contemporary society as a continuum of the past? History museums have collected and interpreted little that reflects the diversity of the American people and their experiences. There is a lack of material related to Afro-Americans, Hispanic Americans, the poor, the immigrant speaking a strange tongue, of the laborer who formed our built environment, or of the social conflict that has marked our national experience. Looking back, it is fair to say that these were sins of omission rather than commission. However, there are important examples of proactive efforts to collect and present materials that fostered a particular vision of America in the belief that such a history would promote a desired social result.

The purposeful use of history is not a revolutionary concept. Interpretations intended to foster a vision of the past and to promote positive social change have been inherent to the founding and activities of history museums in the United States for most of our nation's existence. In the late nineteenth and early twentieth centuries, as a response to waves of new immigration, industrialization, and dramatic social change, civic and business leaders, educators, and patriotic groups fostered the creation of historical societies and museums with the purpose of preserving and promoting an *Americanized* version of the past. Two of today's largest history museums, Colonial Williamsburg and the Henry Ford Museum/Greenfield Village, were established as part of this movement. Thomas J. Wertenbaker, a Princeton historian who for a time joined John D. Rockefeller's effort in Virginia, wrote in 1949:

> It would be difficult to exaggerate the educational value of historical restorations. At a time when the foundations of our country are under attack, when foreign nations are assailing our free institutions with all the misrepresentations which malice can suggest, when they are seconded by a powerful Fifth Column within our borders, when it has become frequent practice to attribute selfish motives to Washington and Jefferson and Hancock and Samuel and John Adams . . . it is of prime importance that we live over again the glorious days which gave us our liberty.[3]

Henry Ford, who had a great deal to do with the social changes transforming America, attempted to create his version of American history near his car factory in Dearborn, Michigan. Its purpose was to promote the idea that small-town America and its values were compatible with industrial America and the values of capitalism. Within a large scale version of Independence Hall, Ford celebrated Western technology and nearby created a village populated by America's historic heroes. Rockefeller chose not to present the story of the slaves who built Williamsburg, nor did Ford feature the workers who fueled the Industrial Revolution.

Commenting on the development of history museums in the United States, Michael Wallace, professor of history at the John Jay College of Criminal Justice, has written:

> History museums . . . in the United States—wittingly or unwittingly— appropriated the past. They did so, first, by presenting particular interpretations. Of course museums cannot be faulted for having read the past selectively. There is no such thing as the past. All history is production—a deliberate selection, ordering, and evaluation of past

events, experiences, and processes . . . museums incorporated selections and silences on such an order that they falsified reality and became instruments of class hegemony.[4]

Henry Ford and John D. Rockefeller consciously viewed their efforts as promoting positive social change. They were presenting historical interpretations they believed Americans needed. In their efforts Ford and Rockefeller were continuing traditions of purposeful history that less well known museum founders had established earlier. Tour the thousands of history museums in the United States and you see exhibitions that present a particular vision of America past and present.

In meeting their social responsibilities, today's history museum directors need first to recognize the historical ideology being transmitted by their own institutions. They also need to ask themselves whether these interpretations are meeting the history needs of their contemporary audiences. Of equal importance is the directors' understanding of the primary role of museums as learning resources where the functions of collecting, preserving, and interpreting are only a means to fulfilling their obligations to society as educators.

*Museums U.S.A.* confirmed that history museum directors have a weak understanding of their responsibilities as educators. It is disconcerting that historical museum directors do not as a group fully understand the role of their museums as learning resources. Education has been the most important characteristic of American museums and those museums' most important service to the public. One hundred years ago, George Brown Goode, Assistant Secretary of the Smithsonian Institution and in charge of the National Museum, presented a paper to the Brooklyn Institute, which at the time was contemplating the establishment of a museum in Brooklyn. The noted zoologist and historian titled his address "The Museum of the Future" and told his audience, "The museum of the past must be set aside, reconstructed, transformed from a cemetery of bric-a-brac into a nursery of living thoughts . . . as one of the principal agencies for the enlightenment of the people." The museum of the future in this democratic land, "should be adapted to the needs of the mechanic, the factory operator, the day laborer, the salesman and the clerk, as much as to those of the professional man and the man of leisure. In short, the public museum is first of all, for the benefit of the public."[5]

In 1909, twenty years after Goode made these remarks, another American museum pioneer, John Cotton Dana, became the head of the Newark Museum Association whose purpose was to establish a museum in Newark, New Jersey. A lawyer by training, Dana prepared for his museum career in public libraries, first in Denver, later at the Springfield Library Association in Massachusetts, and then in Newark. Dana believed that libraries did not exist solely to collect and preserve books. Their importance was rather in serving as an accessible and lively learning resource for the entire community. Dana broadened his vision to include museums and transformed his concepts into reality as director of the Newark Museum.

Between 1917 and 1922 Dana propagated his ideas in a series of small publications with such titles as *The Gloom of Museums: With Suggestions for Removing It, Increasing the Usefulness of Museums,* and *A Museum of Service.* In these, Dana stressed the mission of museums as one of public service: "A good museum attracts, entertains, arouses curiosity, leads to questioning—and thus promotes learning . . . to awaken young and old to interest and inquiry about the world outside themselves."[6] Many of the public programs Dana introduced at the Newark Museum are standard activities of museums today.

In 1942, as the United States entered World War II, a young intern at the Metropolitan Museum of Art addressed the social responsibilities of museums. Theodore Low's *The Museum as Social Instrument* remains today one of the most forceful statements on the social responsibility of museums. Low believed that the "progressive ideas expressed by many of the founders of both our large and small museums testify to the fact that most of them believed that the institutions they were establishing were destined to play an important role in community life."[7] Unfortunately, Low observed, too many museums had thrown that idea out the window. For Low the guiding purpose of museums should be educating the public. He believed that the information transmitted from museums must relate to the public's needs. "In other words," Low wrote, "people must be made to realize how art, science, natural history, or history . . . have a bearing on life as they know it."[8]

Thirty-six years after Low criticized museums for neglecting their educational responsibilities to society, the Commission on the Humanities reported in *The Humanities in American Life* that museums needed to do more to increase the educational value of their exhibitions by placing their messages in a social context accessible to their audiences. The Commission on the Humanities declared:

> Many museum directors identify education as the most important mission of their institutions, recognizing that our cultural heritage should not be kept in storage but should be understood and enjoyed. Museums are uniquely capable of demonstrating the complexity of culture. . . . interpretive exhibits can provide visitors with historical, social, aesthetic, technological and ethnic contexts for contemplating objects. Without such information, understanding and enjoying cultural objects is severely restricted.[9]

Four years after this report was issued, in 1984, another commission—The Commission on Museums for a New Century—prepared a report on the status and future of American museums at the end of the twentieth century. The Commission stated in its *Museums for a New Century:*

> Education in this country—and we use the word broadly to describe the development of knowledge, skills and character—is a pillar of democracy. . . . Museums have long been participants in this national crusade. In fact, many consider public education to be the most significant contribution this country has made to the evolution of the museum concept. . . . If collections are the heart of museums, what we have come to call education—the commitment to presenting objects and ideas in an informative and stimulating way—is the spirit.[10]

The Commission concluded that:

> Museums have a strong and credible position as institutions in society today because they have always assumed a public dimension. The charters of museums founded in the 19th century embraced the Victorian impulse toward social reform. In the 1930s and 1940s museums sought to stress their educational function. The fervent idealism of the 1960s prompted museums even further toward social consciousness.[11]

History museum directors and their institutions can participate more fully in the traditional roles of American museums by recognizing the social importance of historical knowledge and by understanding that collecting and preserving history are only means to transmitting meaningful historical information to their audiences. Knowledge of the past is essential to individual and collective identity. But this understanding of the past is meaningful only if it is placed in the context of the world in which the consumers of that knowledge live. Whether active or passive, interpretations by history museums have a social impact. By necessity, the interpretation is selective. The message being delivered may be pleasant or uncomfortable, but it is never neutral. The goals of the history museum directors are to assure that the interpretation in their exhibitions is based on scholarship and is useful. As Thomas R. Adam wrote in his work *Museums and Popular Culture* in 1939: "Separated from social content a museum is meaningless to anyone but its curators."[12]

The danger of purposeful history is that history museums will replace one historical ideology with another. Museum directors are not without their own cultural prejudices or political views. Directors need to appreciate their own cultural limitations and the limits of the collections they are using to interpret the past. The challenge of history museum directors is not to promote a particular version of the past or vision of the present. It is rather to relate the collections of their institutions to the lives of their museums' audiences and to use these collections to place issues of contemporary importance in historical context. In meeting these responsibilities history museum directors will be confirming the important contribution of history to society and fulfilling their museums' missions as significant learning resources worthy of the attention and support of the communities they serve.

# 4

# The Director as Initiator of Professional Standards and Training

by

## Daniel R. Porter III

DANIEL R. PORTER III has been director of the New York State Historical Association at Cooperstown since 1982 and earlier held the post there of professor and director of the History Museum Studies Program, associated with the State University of New York at Oneonta. Previously he served as director of the Preservation Society of Newport County in Rhode Island, the Ohio Historical Society, and the Historical Society of York in Pennsylvania. He has a B.A. in history from the University of Massachusetts–Amherst, and an M.A. in history from the University of Michigan. He has been a member of the AAM Accreditation Commission and formerly served on the AASLH council. He is the author of several AASLH technical leaflets and reports as well as articles pertaining to museums.

Order and unity in the midst of diversity are evident in this, the earliest American genre painting, the van Bergen overmantle (c. 1732), by John Heaton, of a Dutch farmstead in the lower Hudson Valley. Native and African Americans are seen along with white European colonials in a harmonious, productive, and tidy scene the likes of which all "excellent" museums strive to emulate. Courtesy of the New York State Historical Association, Cooperstown, New York.

*T*his essay makes four statements: that the world of historical museums and agencies is little understood and documented; that in spite of the conservative nature of these organizations, we live in a universe of relentless change; that it does not appear that our field will professionalize in time to meet the increased demands being placed upon it; and that only the directors of these organizations are positioned to accelerate universal adoption of higher institutional standards and greater competency of employees through better training.

If one familiar with the historical museum and agency field today were asked to characterize its present condition, a response probably would not be forthcoming readily. More is publicly known about mystic cults than the operations of repositories of our local and national patrimony. We do know that historical organizations are diverse institutions—formal or "living," introverted or public, exclusive or democratic, shrinelike or dispassionately secular, increasingly commercial, numerous, and uncounted. We know them to be tenacious in maintaining a place in most community rosters of cultural organizations. We are keenly aware that there is no current clearinghouse of their artifactual holdings, but that their archival, manuscript, and published collections are better inventoried and more readily accessible to the diligently inquisitive than ever before. We are embarrassed to realize that there are no comprehensive listings of their end products: Their exhibits, research activities, publications, and the composition and competencies of their staffs are unrecorded. We have little knowledge of their fiscal condition, the numbers and satisfaction levels of their users and clients, and their effectiveness in meeting their missions. History organizations are not well known or understood among themselves or by the public at large.

Benson J. Lossing, Mr. Pictorial Field Book of the last century, was

among the first on the American scene to comment upon museum conditions. Visiting Alexandria, Virginia, in the late 1840s, Lossing singled out the community's history museum for special condemnation. He found the museum, under the mayor's custodianship, closed to the public. Finally gaining admission, he reported he saw important artifacts associated with George Washington jumbled together with "common curiosities covered with dust and cobwebs." "Neglect," he wrote, "is allowing the visible fingers of decay to destroy them [the collections]." No comprehensive picture of nineteenth-century beginnings of historical activities was every detailed by the movement's pioneers.

Laurence Vail Coleman, longtime secretary of the American Association of Museums, was the first to profile our field with intelligent insight. In his *Manual of Small Museums,* Coleman reported that in 1927 there were 1000 in the country, 900 of them "small." Half of all museums were those of colleges and universities, the remainder, private or public, many adjuncts to historical societies in communities of under fifty thousand in the East and Midwest. He found most museums of that day ineffectively administered and in a deplorable state. Some, he noted, were actively operated for the public good and were well supported, but most were not. He attributed the fact that history museums were the most numerous to "pride of ancestry, esteem of place, interest in antiquities, and love of days gone by." We can only guess that these remain the primary motivations for historical organizations.

Coleman believed that many museums and historical societies had been founded to counteract the tendency of Americans to take their notions of the world from books and documents rather than from "culture material." Museums would naturally come to assume warehousing functions with little concern for imparting knowledge, enjoyment, and public service. Few in his day, he said, were able to maintain balance between scholarship and education.

In 1932 the American Association of Museums published its first directory of American museums. It discovered 1,400 of them, only 33 having a budget in excess of $100,000. Among the 781 chartered, nonprofit museums and those created by legislative enactment, 415 were of history. More recent surveys by the Lou Harris organization for the National Endowment for the Arts (1974) and attempts by the Institute of Museum Services and American Association for State and Local History to discover more about museums have been largely quantitative in their findings; but those surveys have determined that history museums remain the most numerous of all types and disciplines, and that they are indeed the museum universe's "poor relations" in budgetary terms. No complete directory of them has been compiled to date, nor has their present condition been documented except for samplings.

For nearly two decades the American Association of Museums has been accrediting museums and allied organizations. A part of the process involves a small group of peers, usually directors, that visits applicant institutions and prepares reports of on-site investigations. Every decade or less accredited museums are required to be revisited by other examiners who similarly record their findings.

Patricia Williams is the accreditation program's current director. In the winter of 1988 she tabulated the findings contained in visiting committee reports of 125 accredited museums and historic sites written from 1985 to 1988. Her unpublished observations based on these reports, a cross section of medium- and large-sized museums for the most part, is the most detailed picture we have of the current condition of this aspect of our field.

Williams found a far healthier and more professional museum community than some observers might expect, a situation substantially improved over what accreditation visitors found during initial on-site inspections in the 1970s. She discovered evidence of intelligent and concerned museum governance with the major weakness being a lack of written or understood chief administrative officer role definitions, the absence of which often indicated problems in other areas of museum operations. She found peer respect (gratuitous or not) on the part of examiners for museum staffs that resulted in high marks for dedication, professionalism, and training; but she found in the reports that a critical shortage of curators exists, a deficiency that translates into program problems. She found that curatorial staffs frequently lack knowledge of the intellectual content of their collections, while collections housekeeping was vastly improving. "The caretaking function has outstripped the educative," she observed.

Fiscal management she found to be a problem in only 2 percent of the 125 museums whose reports she surveyed, but the need for more financial support was frequently cited. Museums appear to her to be "the most fiscally conservative and tightly managed" of all cultural organizations. Only in the past decade has the obligation to invest in collections been recognized. She also noted that museums with balanced budgets or with surpluses are allowing their collections to deteriorate and are doing precious little research and interpretation among collections.

More and better exhibit space is the greatest physical need museums have, she determined. All museums in her study had space and atmospheric condition deficiencies. Behind-the-scenes spaces such as storage areas, offices, and labs were generally the most neglected, while she found that capital improvements were routinely made for parking and public services areas. "American museums are bursting at the seams, but they are doing it in a dignified way," she concludes.

Her review of accreditation reports similarly revealed that collections record keeping was frequently in need of improvement, followed by more complete and accurate cataloging, needs tied directly to the shortage of competent curators. Resource management is receiving top attention today, while research and educational activities lag behind. Poor object handling practices were frequently found among curatorial staffs, and periodic collections condition reports were often deficient or nonexistent. Measures to protect physical plants and collections from risk is a high museum priority today.

Museum end products were the areas of greatest need, her review indicates. Exhibit design, content, labels, graphics, and object arrangement and mounting were found in many museums to be primitive and unsatisfactory, often lacking conceptual or even logical arrangement. Exhibits in many instances are prepared without thorough research and a knowledge of how people learn. Museum public programming was rarely scrutinized by accreditation examiners, and when it was, no perceptive evaluative judgments were made. Williams found that accredited museums, overall, probably one fourth of all museums that meet the AAM's basic definition, are doing very well; but she found that there was little evidence that the issue of developing a broader knowledge base for public use programs and collections is being addressed adequately by museums. This intimate glimpse into the private lives of accredited museums lends a measure of understanding of their currently accepted standards of performance of charter purposes and legislative mandates.

The only standards subscribed to by a segment of the historical field are those for museums adopted in 1969 for accreditation purposes by the American Association of Museums after nearly a decade of definition debate. A museum must be organized or duly constituted with stated responsibilities; be permanent and nonprofit; knowledgeable in the utilization of its collections for elucidation and enjoyment; and have at least one paid employee with command of an appropriate body of knowledge and the ability to make decisions consonant with those of his or her peers. Museums must own, secure, utilize, and care for tangible objects related to their stated purposes and keep adequate records of those objects. Finally, museums have to be open regular hours convenient to the public.

The application of the most basic of these standards to the field in 1974 by the Harris-NEA survey resulted in the discovery that there were at that time 683 history museums in the United States, 37 percent of the total museum universe with at least one paid staff, open to the public regularly, and having an annual budget of over $12,000. These 683 museums are only a fraction of the number of those historical museums listed in current directories. It would appear, then, that as America prepares to enter the twenty-first century, the standards of performance of an elite group of history museums and sites are somewhat higher than they had been earlier in the century, but that a majority has failed to date to meet the most elemental of professional standards.

As for manuscript and archival depositories and historical libraries, historic preservation organizations, publications departments, and other agency program areas, little is known of their individual and collective performance standards; and there is no attempt to monitor or record their relative levels of performance largely owing to the fiercely independent, sometimes contrary, stances of many of these organizations. Sincerity remains the basic evaluative yardstick our field chooses to employ. If, indeed, as Lois Shepard wrote in her Institute of Museum Services' Tenth Annual Report, "Museums are America's identity . . . composed of our values, our standards, our beliefs, our accomplishments, and our aspirations—past and present," then indeed that identity is not in very sharp focus.

The very word *standards* conjures up frightened and bristly opposition from those who are expected to live up to them. Critics of standards, particularly those that seem to be imposed from the outside, bemoan the uniformity they are believed to inflict upon those who conform to them. The application of standards can destroy their adherents' ability to realize their individual potentiality, some argue. Acceptable standards are usually vague and are applied through a process of self-examination and collegial review that shields the subjects from embarrassment and criticism.

There are three kinds of standards that are applicable to the historical field. The first are those of *structure*—how the museum, site, or agency is organized to accomplish its legally mandated mission. The second, those of *procedure*—what are the organization's practices in the performance of its goals and objectives and in the conservation of its assets. And finally, those of *outcomes*—of what quality and utility are the organization's end products to their users.

State laws relating to nonprofit corporations have the most direct application to structural and procedural standards. But this body of law in each state is not specifically written for historical institutions and gives little guidance to attorneys general or to the subjects of the laws on the levels of performance expected of them and the mode of their operation as they serve public interests in exchange for privileged tax exempt status. State laws and local ordinances that establish historical agencies, sites, and museums, and prescribe ethical standards for their employees, offer no guidelines for level of performance or usefulness of end products.

Federal and state granting agencies in the last two decades have effectively forced higher standards on their recipients and, in some cases, have literally meddled in the internal affairs of their clients in order to achieve higher structural and procedural standards. The New York State Council on the Arts, for example, increasingly requires historical society and museum directors, who also serve as trustees, to relinquish their seats on the governing body to qualify for council grants. In spite of this godfatherly attention, there are few good surveys of the outcomes of this guided fiscal assistance and the relative merit of grant program end products. On October 19, 1987, a day otherwise remembered for the disastrous stockmarket plunge of 508 points, Laura Werner, assistant attorney general for the state of New York, told seminarians convened by the Metropolitan Museum of Art that "Government imposes few standards on museums. . . . States' attorneys general are going to have to use professional and accountability yardsticks developed by the American Association of Museums. There are no other." She reported that most complaints against museums received by her office pertain to waste of assets, poor collections management procedures and practices, and tax and investment problems.

Public expectations of historical organization performance have traditionally been low. As a result there have not been many efforts to increase legal performance requirements. The public's relations with historical groups are voluntary in nature and have little effect on public health, welfare, and safety except for the *quality-of-life* doctrine. The public, therefore, makes fewer demands on history organizations among all those that serve the commonweal.

Governing bodies rarely take the initiative to impose internally higher structural, procedural, and outcome standards within their own institutions. Those who hold responsible staff positions are the primary initiators of higher standards and in so doing ideally prod their governors to adopt policies that help to raise standards incrementally. Standards lag behind the natural norm in those organizations whose professional staffs fail to demand higher performance levels. Only as accreditation pressures, voluntarily accepted by museums, are applied do we find museum boards adopting policies that refine structure and prescribe procedure. Few organizations have reached a level of professionalism to adopt standards that relate to the quality of end products and outcomes.

It's impossible to list those structural, procedural, and outcome standards that are universally accepted and acceptable by our diverse field today, because there appear to be none. Only the museum accreditation process has over the years developed a few standards in addition to those contained in the basic definition of a museum. These include approved delegations of appropriate authority and responsibility by the governing authority to the chief administrative officer and staff, and include the existence of approved policies that specify collections management practices, and maintenance and utilization of facilities and collections in ways that protect and preserve those assets. Beyond these very basic, nonqualitative standards, there are no guidelines other than the definition of what a museum is, no commandments other than pertinent law, no required ethical dictates, and no acceptable, qualitative measurements for end products. Laissez faire runs rampant in Clio's fiefdom.

Debate continues over whether or not the imposition of standards on historical organizations by outside professional and governmental bodies diminishes institutional autonomy, dampens innovation, and fosters conformity. Should professional historians from academe critique museum exhibits and site restorations for their validity and effectiveness just as they review scholarly publications of those same historical agencies and museums? Are the academics qualified to make judgments about material culture end products, a field in which they are often undereducated and unsympathetic? Users of historical organization services and products have, some claim, the greatest right to evaluate, to help insure quality control and the maintenance of higher performance and outcome standards even though these users often are the least qualified to make assessments. Should not there be some duly constituted body representative of users and the public that can furnish assurances that standards are being set and met by the historical community?

The study of history makes none of its practitioners prognosticators. The historian's crystal ball is as cloudy as that of any other field. About the only way the future may be glimpsed is through the study of current trends, many of which will have culminated years hence in firm, new directions. Change complicates efforts in our field to improve effectiveness and efficiency as well as to attain higher standards. Scanning the horizon for signals of change is about the only way we can fathom the future effectively even though cultural, technological, and natural interferences beyond our control tend to prevent predictable repetitions of patterns.

If we read the tea leaves correctly, structured standards to which historical organizations adhere today will continue to evolve toward greater democratization in governance. Governing boards and public museum administrators will gradually adopt limited terms of office for trustees and advisors who increasingly will be elected or appointed from competitive slates. Bodies so constituted place greater demands upon their directors as those who govern are elected or appointed on the basis of platform planks, proponents of which insist on their adoption during shortened tenures. Directors will have to master new competencies if they are to serve their boards effectively.

Those who staff museums will become more militant over low salaries, inadequate fringe benefits, day care for infants, and other employee needs. These pressures will require better fiscal management of museums in order to stretch inflated dollars. Governing bodies will, as a result, seek more highly trained and competent directors and personnel who will reorganize operations that will become more responsive to increased internal and external demands. Staffs that want greater compensation will simply have to be better performers. The typical historical organization employee of the next century will be a specialist either in an academic or operational capacity. That specialist will command professional insights and knowledge at a much earlier point in his or her career than at present. Greater fiscal effectiveness and mastery of technological proficiencies will be demanded of employees. Historical organizations may no longer enjoy the luxury of low productivity. Governance will insist upon greater efficiency.

Changing demographic and travel patterns, how leisure time is used, coupled with new and exciting forms of amusement, will prompt our institutions that depend upon admission revenues to respond more promptly to public interests; the result will be a widening gap between organizations that recognize social and cultural needs and those that do not. An example will be a new kind of museum, the history center. In imitation of science centers that have deaccessioned their collections and use some of them as educational tools, history centers will relieve themselves of the increasingly costly function of collections management and will fill their buildings with theme park wizardry and hokum. Robotry, electronic participation devices, "rides" in reproduced historic forms of locomotion—a mechanical bull in every western history center—will become the norm for this new breed of museum; while others that choose to retain traditional programming will increasingly become artifact libraries where wordsmiths will employ electronic cataloging and information retrieval to interpret artifacts and documents that themselves are secreted in dark, environmentally controlled vaults safe from the gaze and touch of the inquisitive. The medium, as has been predicted, will become the message.

As fossil fuel on our planet is exhausted early in the next century, the energy hogs we know our libraries, archives, and museums to be will require redesign or retrofitting for collections preservation at more reasonable cost. This will mean that the inefficient, brutal, concrete buildings designed in the last three decades to awe an admiring public will be modified or replaced by energy efficient structures, less monumental and more functional in nature.

Procedural standards in our organizations will respond both to those of structure and outcomes. Historical staffs, increasingly specialized, will embrace even larger numbers of other professions which will introduce new processes and procedures that will be carefully codified so that, at long last, precedent will become equally or more important than innovation, untested whimsical practices shunned in favor of cost-consciousness. The ethics of historical administration will assume new importance as a tax-burdened public becomes increasingly aware of paying the assessments of the exempt. The public trust concept will be forcibly brought home as class action suits may force cultural organizations to be less playthings of the few and private clubs, and more productive, competent, and a part of mainstream society. Revenues generated from noncharter purpose activities will unquestionably be taxed by states and the federal government in reaction to the competition they offer to taxed businesses. Quirkiness that marks the operations of many of our organizations will similarly give way as our smaller institutions become a part of central cultural society.

New organizational structures and procedures will permit more successful historical organization outcomes. Interpretation is the challenge of the future. As our organizations improve the quality and extent of their programming and generate greater amounts of organized source materials, comparison and contrast will become the new historical processes that result in better interpretation. Classes of objects and concepts about them will be formulated to replace concentration on artifacts as unica. Those who work in our organizations will gain the ability to visualize for others interrelationships that to date have escaped the comprehension of many of our peers. Technology and electronics will be our handmaiden as we reach out to serve the new *lifelong learning society* that will have fully blossomed in the next century. The over-fifty age group is growing at twice the population rate. With more than two decades of life expectancy after retirement, the gray generation will increasingly seek answers to questions about origins, causes, and connections, and will respond to insightful, penetrating analyses that new interpretations will furnish.

The record of humankind that historical organizations preserve will take on for many of our users new forms of appreciation, particularly the search for heroes and heroines. The public will increasingly identify with personalities whose contributions will be memorialized in more halls of fame than we care to count. Roots-questioning minorities, particularly, will seek to enshrine and revere their leaders who are emerging today. "It's not the game, but who plays it that counts." The social, political, artistic, and military playing fields of America will furnish us interpretation inspiration, as have those of athletics and amusement.

Education at all levels will retain its back-to-basics emphasis as America struggles into the next century to regain some of its lost greatness. Historical organizations will more readily form partnerships with schools to provide curriculum-friendly learning opportunities for the young. The needs of special segments of society—these that are gifted, learning disabled, underprivileged, physically handicapped, minorities, or infirm—will be met as never before by our organizations as their assets, increasingly recognized as being held in public trust, are tapped as newly discovered humanistic resources.

In another generation, history museums will begin to conceptualize the real world, a process that will revolutionize our end products. More self-confident directors and their staffs will summon the courage to present subjects that formerly had been considered too controversial for the halls of historydom. Burning issues like sex, disease, religion, environment, privacy, and bigotry, sometimes in the name of truth, at other times for effect, will become as commonplace in galleries as platitudinous patriotic piety had been of yore. Consider the museum and historical library of the future more idea centers than repositories of things preserved for their intrinsic value.

New standards of organization, process, and outcome will demand competent directors above all else. Slowly and grudgingly, those with disciplinary vested interests will give ground to a new order that puts thoroughgoing competency ahead of allegiances, blind or rational. If indeed work in historical organizations constitutes a profession, then the tenets and standards of professionalism peculiar to our field must be more widely accepted and practiced. Laurence Vail Coleman recognized as early as 1939 that "learning as well as skill, pursued for society's benefit, has other than fiscal measures of success, assumes responsibility through its practitioner *as a group* for ideals, objectives, and discipline" (italics mine). He meant standards. "Practitioners," he maintained, "must possess both learning and technique."

Basic questions of professionalism in the historical field have been argued since the 1930s. Issues debated to this very day deal largely with training—should those who work in historical organizations have specific training? Who should offer it? Of what should the training consist? Higher standards that will be required of our field in the next century will generate the need for a new breed of director, curator, librarian, and archivist, one equipped as never before to lead the field as it meets its new challenges. Academically trained art historians, natural scientists, archaeologists, and anthropologists have no difficulty straddling the worlds of museum and academe because their disciplines utilize material culture and specimens. But professional historians are trained only to use documentary evidence in pursuit of their quest for truth. This causes material world alienation. The late University of Wisconsin historian, William B. Hesseltine, speaking at the 1957 American Association for State and Local History annual meeting in Columbus, Ohio, said, "The historian can ask the manuscript questions through internal criticism to extract meaning from it. But the artifact is incapable of response." The opinion caused nary a ripple in the audience. Hesseltine was artifactually illiterate, a condition historical organization directors must never be allowed to suffer.

Bias against the artifact on the part of historians has produced the attitude, emanating from academic sources, that those who specialize in material culture studies and in technique are deemed to be intellectually inferior to those who pursue what are described as disciplinary studies. This mind-set has had the effect of denigrating museum end products such as historic restorations, exhibits, and published collection catalogs concerning which there is little critical activity. Similarly, popular history as it is published by our societies and agencies goes unrecognized, as academic historians unsuccessfully take a contrary tack by trying to make quasi-historians of amateurs.

The traditional training route of those employed by historical organizations has been education in a related academic discipline as offered by an institution of higher learning, followed by an internship or apprenticeship in a museum or historical agency. In this way, academic learning is combined with guided practice to create a balanced practitioner. This mode of preparation for work in our field is now being seriously challenged for a variety of reasons. Governing bodies are requiring better prepared directors and staff members who do not have to learn their skills on the job at the employer's expense. If efficiency and cost effectiveness are to be improved, as they must, salaried and fringed novices have become a luxury for the prudent employer. The old saw so often heard: "Give me a trained historian and I'll make a curator (or director, or registrar, or archivist, or librarian) of him or her" is no longer a justifiable training plan. It simply costs too much.

But more important than dollars is the growing belief among historical organization trustees and administrators that the directorial role can be called a profession only when the practitioners of that role are required to have formal training before they enter the job marketplace. If standards in the field are to be measurably improved, a true profession must be developed, a condition that has to be forced to be attained. Only when applicants are required by employers to have formal preparation that consists both of mastery of a discipline and a body of techniques will a profession emerge that sets improved standards for itself.

Professional schools create professions, not employers. The learning process is composed equally of education and training. Ideally, a professional is well grounded in both academic disciplinary studies and in the body of techniques that each profession must utilize to attain its

. Those who work in historical organizations have to be schooled ү scholarship, we all agree. In addition, the learner must obtain guided practice in appropriate techniques, learn the specialized vocabulary, and acquire the ability to organize and communicate information effectively.

If education and training are both required of the balanced historical organization director and employee, who appropriately offers each form of instruction? Traditionally, learning in a discipline has been the responsibility of colleges and universities, while museums and agencies have furnished apprentice or internship opportunities where skills and techniques are mastered. But at this writing, over fifty colleges and universities are believed to be offering some of both kinds of learning, history and anthropology departments being the most numerous sponsors of public history and museological education. The typical department alters the titles of a few of its courses, hires a museum or agency director in an adjunct status to offer a management course, and emphasizes its warmed-over minor as a means of placing larger numbers of its graduates. Those prepared under this regimen do not in most cases appear to meet the needs of a professionalizing field whose practitioners must be thoroughly acquainted with the traditions, ethics, practices, obligations, and lore associated with a true profession and be respectful of its traditions. Nor are these programs equipped to formulate and propose the adoption of standards for a field about which faculties have little or no understanding.

Compounding the problem is the lack of recruitment sophistication exhibited by museum and agency employers. Representatives of lay governing boards who comprise search committees for directors are often unable to describe and recognize the qualities they seek in their applicants. Employers are imprecise about the responsibilities and authority they are willing to delegate to directors, as they are foggy about basic institutional mission and end product criteria. Since neither the educational institutions that produce many of the applicants, nor the employing organizations that use the human product, really know the objectives and needs of the other and of the field in general, professional progress is stymied, standards are not universally established, and employees are frustrated both by deficient career preparation and by diminished expectations on the job.

The general failure of those who attempt to prepare students for a career in our field and of those who govern our organizations is their inability to define and recognize competency in both methodology as well as in academic learning. This lack of leadership remains the most formidable barrier to the development of standards and the improvement of practices in our field. Both the AAM and AASLH have half-heartedly appointed committees in the decades of the seventies and eighties to formulate criteria and standards for historical agency and museum training and sought to encourage self-evaluation by programs that offer this training. The efforts may be characterized as half-hearted because the governing councils of both associations, as well as the field itself, remain, except for a few lonely voices in the wilderness, largely uncommitted to improving standards through better training.

No institutions offering training opportunities for our field are known to be aggressively pursuing opportunities for minorities and the handicapped, the cultural exiles of our society, who are without roots in their new home or whose roots are institutionally demeaned or ignored. Historical activities sensitize the rootless and offer them a feeling of identity with the past that simultaneously furnishes them promise for the future. But cultural exiles they will remain as long as representatives of each minority or special group are not encouraged actively, or are denied access to, professional practice.

The quest for improved standards in any professionalizing field must solve humanely the problem of those who, long on experience but short on training and competency, occupy key positions to which they have risen simply by surviving longer. Those who lack the intellectual capacity and appropriate education must either be given the opportunity to improve through continuing education opportunities or be outplaced as painlessly as possible.

Ours remains a field of little pecuniary promise. There are only two basic conditions for seeking a career in history—lacking the training or ability to do anything else or dedication to a pursuit that offers intense satisfaction. Neither of these motivations are sufficient to transform a polyglot field into a true profession with high standards and a well-trained and motivated professional work force. The challenge before the leaders of our field, the museum and agency directors, is to organize nationally, formally or informally, in order to force, through control of the job marketplace, better learning opportunities for all presently in the field and those seeking to enter it. Only in this way will standards improve and professionalization occur. Mechanisms exist today for directors to force academe to produce a more competent graduate for work in our organizations. Directors are ideally positioned to lead the change for improved standards in how they organize and implement their efforts. They control the hiring mechanisms of their organizations, and they decree qualifications for their own jobs and those of their staffs. Only the will to do so has been lacking, or mere advocacy is thought to be an acceptable substitute for organized, effective action.

Deeply rooted in "good-old-boyism," we directors have been more concerned with appearances than competency in and among our own

ranks and those of our staffs. We have too often learned to accept medi-
ocrity as the norm. That's why our tenures are ever shorter, seven years
or less, it appears on average. Governance increasingly is aware of inadequate performance and standards and is not above ordering change,
only to discover the replacement may not be the equal of the predecessor. From better learning opportunities come higher standards of performance that in turn yield improved outcomes. Until directors
collectively come to this realization, until they organize to effect change,
our field will remain an ill-defined, introverted, too often self-serving,
disorganized, unproductive, disparate collection of institutions, both
large and small, that suffer from their own inability to address the challenge of change effectively.

# 5

# The Director's Role in Collections Development, Management, and Conservation

by

Lynne F. Poirier–Wilson

Lʏɴɴᴇ F. Poɪʀɪᴇʀ–Wɪʟsoɴ has been vice president for collections at the Strong Museum, Rochester, New York, since 1982. She was director of the Bucks County Historical Society, Doylestown, Pennsylvania, from 1979 to 1982, prior to which she was chief curator of the society's Mercer Museum and associate curator of technology and internship administrator at the Rochester Museum and Science Center. She holds a B.A. in English from the State University of Potsdam, New York, and has participated in several mid-career museum training programs. She has been a member of the AAM Council and the steering committee of the AASLH Common Agenda for History Museums project and is the immediate past president of the Mid-Atlantic Association of Museums. Poirier–Wilson collaborated on the original publication and organized the current revision of *Nomenclature for Museum Cataloging,* published in 1978.

Mercer Museum cataloger, March 1989. It is the people who will develop and care for our collections. Managing collections requires people skills as well as organizational skills. Courtesy of the Mercer Museum of the Bucks County Historical Society, Doylestown, Pennsylvania.

*T*here is an apocryphal story that roams the halls of Buck County's Mercer Museum. In the early 1970s a visiting museum scholar told the newly hired director that were he in charge of the Mercer collection, he would find a shady tree on a sunny day, contemplate what was to be done with the "stuff," and probably shoot himself. Whether or not the provenance of that particular tale can ever be documented, many history museum directors, curators, and registrars experience similar feelings when they confront the overwhelming masses of "stuff" in their own institutions.

Although history museums and historical societies generally started later than art and science collections, the numbers of objects multiplied on a grand scale—all without the benefit of a systematic method to evaluate their worth to the museum, to the community, or, if applicable, to the nation. As collections grew, history museums became community, regional, or national attics; knowledge about the objects was often lost, and control of them was sometimes never achieved at all.

How have we come to inhabit this situation? Some of our organizations arose from collections amassed to worship an ancestor or a community. Some expressed emotional ties to particular military struggles. Some were the material formulation of an individual or collective emotional response to an object or group of objects, some a collector's legacy. No matter how they began, our museums have grown in multitudinous and sometimes bizarre ways. Fear of losing an object that might hold meaning for a particular community, collecting in a wholesale and indiscriminate way (the vacuum cleaner method), and fear of offending possibly influential donors have helped us heap up all that "stuff." For many years, the personal tastes and interests of those who held power, be they volunteer or paid staff, also held sway over the collections of many institutions. As one person left and another became involved, the focus of the collection often changed as a result. Our institutions' original intentions have become complicated by such shifts in focus as well as by the sheer number of things collected.

Professional concern about the state of history museum collections has been constant over the past fifty years or so. Laurence Vail Coleman stated: "Many [history] museums, including a few of some size, have hardly anything of consequence. Others are choked with irrelevant material. Nearly every museum has some stuff it would be better off without, and some are almost hopelessly cluttered up" [*The Museum in America* 3 vols. (Washington, D.C.: American Association of Museums, 1939. Reprint 1977), 236]. Forty-five years later, in 1984, the Commission on Museums for a New Century made collections its highest priority. "First there are pressing needs with regard to the growth, organization, and care of museum collections. Museum staff, trustees, and supporters must turn closer attention to the current and future conditions of the objects that are the heart of our museums" [*Museums for a New Century,* (Washington, D.C.: AAM, 1984)].

In the broadest sense collection management is no more than exercising control over a domain. As a concept it is of fairly recent origin, and it simply entails knowing what we have, why we have it, where we have it, how we care for it, and what we plan to do with it. If the collection is the "heart" of our organizations, then the management of that asset is part of its brain.

The museum director is the person charged with making that brain think about collections care, one of the many priorities that compete for attention. Sometimes amidst worrying about the hole in the roof, the shortfall projected at year's end, the staff's seemingly low morale, the new trustees' orientation, the upcoming building project, the IMS grant deadline, the new exhibit opening, the fund raiser scheduled next month, the large dead tree very close to the visitors' entrance, the unkind letter to the editor, the collections—those quiet collections—get pushed to the back of the active file. This is particularly true if those collections are disorganized and if every decision regarding them is ad hoc. However, those quiet collections are a major reason for our institution's being, and as directors we must force our boards and our staffs to push them forward.

## What We Have and Why We Have It

Inventories and surveys can help us determine what is in the collections, but they cannot tell us why we have them. Only a mission statement can answer that question. Although some may believe that a mission statement is etched in marble at the entrance to the building, in truth collections and the mission statement influence each other. If we know our collections and understand their strengths and weaknesses, we are better able to articulate the basis for our own mission; and an agreement upon mission statement can help a museum manage its collections intellectually.

Many years ago the Bucks County Historical Society, the parent organization of the Mercer Museum, was struggling with a mission statement and the scope of the Mercer collection. The Mercer Museum had been established by Henry Mercer, an anthropologist, as a comparative study collection of the tools that built this nation, from blacksmith to carpenter, and from weaver to teacher. The mass of the collections fit into the broad concept of tools. But other objects with Bucks County provenance and importance had been incorporated into the collections and often into the exhibits. The concern was how to mesh them, or if such amalgamation was even a feasible plan. A new building dedicated to Bucks County history was, at the time, out of the question. Through a series of sometimes heated discussions, a rationale was formulated for the institution. Could the story of the tools that built the nation be told properly if there were not exhibited some products that those tools had wrought?

Much of the Bucks County material consisted of collections most generally defined as decorative arts. These decorative arts objects were often the products of a particular craft or trade. Although Mercer's collection was national in scope, could the organization not use Bucks County as a microcosm for study? In many ways the outcome of those meetings helped clarify acquisition procedures for the society and allowed it to collect local historical materials as well as those of national significance. Such discussions and the delineated statement also helped both trustees and staff to understand the worth of the objects and to begin thinking about future collection and resource expansion. A knowledge of the collections and a recognition of their importance to the organization was essential to the process of discussing the museum's mission intelligently.

Mission statements should be reviewed every few years. If it is clear that the institution is functioning well and in accordance with its mission, nothing more than an update and information session may be needed. But if it is muddled or the museum has naturally moved beyond its boundaries, it will need refinement. Perhaps one of the most exciting outcomes of such a refining process is that a statement brings about a measure against which the institution can be assessed. In organizations where products are not easily defined and "success" is often not quantifiable, a standard by which operations may be evaluated gives a sense of direction to both employees and supporters.

If a director works for an institution that is large enough to have paid staff, the responsibility for the collections has usually been delegated to a curator, registrar, collections manager, or some combination of those positions. The director's responsibility, among others, is to be aware of the organization as a whole and to give institutional perspective to the collection and to collection management. If, however, the director is the lone professional or perhaps even the lone employee, then both the responsibility for the collections and the institutional picture will reside in one individual. In such a case, a diplomatic use of board, community, and consultant resources can aid in bringing that broader perspective to the organization.

The museum's mission also charts the course of collection development, both in terms of the types of objects to be collected and the ways in which those objects are to be used. Because much of history is still taught from the viewpoint of the written word, history museums have in the past lacked a meaningful philosophy that would help define relevant categories of objects. For the lack of any alternative, many history museums have attempted to graft classification schemes used in art museums onto history collections. Although such categories as style, maker, or period are useful to us, they lack historical perspective based on theme, context, and use; and they often encourage us to consider ourselves as stepchildren to art museums. Although more material culture programs have evolved in recent years, there are still not enough practitioners to go around. This has left many history museums struggling to define their collections and set boundaries for them without benefit of much scholarly comment.

Because of the work of Robert Chenhall and hundreds of individuals across the United States and Canada, a system now exists to categorize historical objects. Whether individually one agrees with the concept of function as a method for organizing objects, *The Revised Nomenclature for Museum Cataloging* (Nashville: AASLH, 1988 ) is available to help sort out collections, to establish a systematic hierarchy, and to give names to the objects that inhabit our storage and exhibition areas. Deciding upon a method of classification is only another step in maintaining collection control. Thinking about the collections in the broadest possible terms will allow us to use them in ways that will promote an appreciation of history, as well as an active interest and an enhanced sense of excitement about it.

As the institutional overseer, the director helps develop institutional themes and to establish criteria for collection development. A collection develops in two ways—through the acquisition of objects and through the disposal of objects. Formulating a series of questions that can be used during both of these processes will clarify why an object should be acquired or why an object should or should not remain in the collections. If a museum in a rural setting, for example, wishes to focus on agriculture and its effect on community life, themes such as transportation, agrarianism, disasters, commerce, foodways, geography, individualism, and mechanization will help to identify particular areas of significance to collection development. Other more specifically object-oriented criteria, such as naming the object, establishing provenance, and formally delineating the object's relationship to the institution's mission, should follow a theme discussion.

Used in tandem, the exploration of historical themes and association and the examination of questions about the specific object will place the object in context and enhance its value to the collection. An object should never be acquired or disposed of without benefit of such discussion. Although a director need not see each and every object acquired, a consistent review of the methodology used should be considered a top priority. Inventories and surveys can help determine how to group existing collections according to themes. Such groupings often help in terms of developing comprehensive exhibitions and programs for the future as well as defining collection gaps for the present.

## How We Care for Objects

Developing collections is not an end in itself. The care of those collections is an equal responsibility of museum directors. Ironically, as collections have become more orderly, their physical needs have become more apparent. History museum objects are often in a state of disrepair. Funding problems, poor storage conditions, the sheer number of objects, and the lack of recognition that common objects require as much care as rare objects have all contributed to this disrepair.

Federal and private funding sources have recognized these conservation needs and now offer broad help in the care of the collections. Although most history museums cannot afford to put conservators on staff, consultants can help by surveying collections, recommending controls and equipment for storage and exhibition areas, suggesting conservation priorities, and finally by actually treating objects. A director should be able to articulate conservation needs so that a broad public will understand what kind and extent of care is needed to maintain museum collections. Knowledge of the organization's budgetary capabilities, its interpretive focus, its community resources, and its mission will help the director work with staff to establish conservation priorities and to seek funding for such priorities.

## What We Plan To Do With Museum Objects

Directors have other concerns directly related to collection management. A range of legal and ethical issues affect our collections, and directors ought to attend such specialized seminars as the ALI–ABA course on "Legal Problems of Museum Administration" and be familiar with such books as Marie Malaro's *A Legal Primer on Managing Museum Collections* (Washington, D.C.: Smithsonian Institution Press, 1985). Understanding these legal and ethical areas will aid in developing those policies that govern collection care. Thoughtful statements on acquisition, deaccession, conservation, inventory, use of objects, incoming and outgoing loans, access, insurance, and abandoned objects will spell out our institutions' commitment to the collections. Most institutions would not consider adopting personnel policies without legal review. Collections should be considered in the same way and be subject to similar scrutiny.

Many museums have already developed collection policies and will make copies of them available upon reasonable request. Each institution, however, is different. Although others' policies are a starting point for thinking about one's organization, each institution must develop its own set of policies that spring from and reflect internal and external needs. Directors can help keep policy development on track by focusing on the museum's mission and delineating how the institution functions within its community and among its peers.

## Conclusion

As history museums enter the twenty-first century, they need to take stock of where they have been, where they are now, and where they wish to go. A director will want to keep the board, the staff, and the community aware of the strengths, the needs, and the mission of the institution. Developing or refining a mission, establishing thematic ways to view the collection, classifying objects, developing carefully delineated collections policies, and establishing a solid conservation philosophy and methodology will help to keep the "stuff" manageable and usable. Everything cannot be done in a few days or weeks or months. Recognizing the needs and developing a logical plan are first steps in tackling collection management problems. A director who guides and supports both staff and the board through this long process, however, may never have to find that shady tree on a sunny day.

# 6

# The Director's Role in Exhibition and Educational Interpretation

by

Craig A. Gilborn

CRAIG A. GILBORN has been director of the Adirondack Museum, Blue Mountain Lake, New York, since 1972. Previously he held positions as executive director of the Delaware State Arts Council, in the Education Division of the H. F. duPont Winterthur Museum in Delaware, and in the Programs Division of the Virginia Museum of Fine Arts, Richmond. He has an M.A. from the University of Delaware (Winterthur Program in Early American Culture) and a B.A. in English from Michigan State University. He has written numerous articles and books on Adirondack region and other subjects and has been involved in a half dozen major exhibitions and research projects undertaken by the museum. He is past president of the Mid-Atlantic Association of Museums and the New York State Association of Museums, and is a trustee of the Shelburne Museum in Vermont.

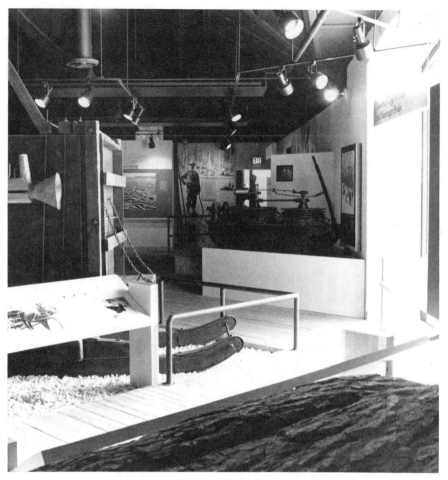

*Work in the Woods: Logging the Adirondacks,* a permanent exhibition at the Adirondack Museum that opened in two stages, in 1988 and 1989, in a building of 5,200 square feet that had undergone extensive renovations in 1987. Courtesy of the Adirondack Museum, Blue Mountain Lake, New York.

*T*he old woman who lived in a shoe did not discriminate: she gave her children "some broth without any bread" and she "whipped them *all* soundly and put them to bed." Today's museum director, perhaps abetted by workshop exposure, is inclined to treat staff with the same evenhandedness as that harassed lady. Day-to-day pressures dispose the museum director to accept the wisdom of acting as though one staff member were as important as the next, for nothing orders a director's priorities more quickly than a plugged toilet or a computer that has crashed. Broth to the plumber, broth to the curator.

## Confusing Means With Ends

This egalitarian spirit is fine in the workaday world. But indifference or confusion as to the difference between means and ends must lead the museum to lose purpose and to drift. Does it just *seem* as though administrators are predisposed to aver, with a hint of pride, that curators are spoiled and inhabit ivory towers but that they are "treated like anybody else on staff"? (Few dare speak glibly of museum educators for fear of being obligated to visit them in the trenches.) In recent years I have found myself wondering about the national confusion of style for substance, translated in the museum as the replacement of institutional ends by managerial means, with the consequence that the museum must eventually be informed and shaped less by the pursuit and communication of knowledge than by the self-serving values of the bureaucrat.

The product of the museum is not management; it is preservation and knowledge. Yet managerial values—and all organizations need good management—have come to outnumber those who speak for traditional museum purposes. Those belittling remarks subvert the meaning and purpose of the museum itself; their intent is not innocent when delivered by administrators who may be compensating for the inadequacy of their knowledge.

From the foregoing, I would submit the following proposition: *Museum collections are ends and all else are means.* In other words, without collections and curatorial and educational functions there can be no true museum; the concept of the museum embodies collections and people possessing skills and knowledge about their care and interpretation.

The modern museum progressively obscures matters accepted as articles of faith by earlier generations of museum directors, nearly all of whom were specialists in a field of knowledge. While we cannot go back (and would not even if it were possible), the mantle worn by the museum director from that earlier era remains unaltered. The director must be the advocate for the museum as the preserver of the material and recorded heritage of a people or the environment. From this premise it will be seen that among the many things that the modern museum does, some are qualitatively more important than others. Collections are nearest to the museum's purpose; little should compromise their care and augmentation, as much for posterity's claim to the museum as for our own. Education and interpretation are secondary to collections only when a choice has to be made, as when art was crated and stored in caves in Great Britain during the Second World War. All else that takes place in the museum—and the list gets longer with each year (which justifies repetition of the purposes of the museum)—are means to collections and interpretive ends. These instrumentalities include public relations, development, shop and restaurant operations, personnel, maintenance, and administration.

One must be realistic. An experienced development officer is likely to command one of the highest salaries on a museum's payroll. Such "real world" allowances of the market place should not lead the museum director to re-order the institution's priorities, to allocate resources favoring the obvious at the expense of the less obvious. Always important, money has become so conspicuous to validation and success that one asks how the museum director will resist when others better equipped to resist, such as the presidents of colleges with nationally ranked sports teams, confess failure.

Notwithstanding, the director must guard against cynicism and the meretricious lest he and his successors find themselves presiding over a hollow shell. For the ancients the museum was a repository of the known and a fountainhead of inspiration. This notion informs the museum and therefore nourishes it. But the light is not inextinguishable. The museum's growing resemblance to the department store and country club as stratagems for survival is no cause to pursue the cheap and easy as though they were virtues.

### The "History-Is-Not-Art-or-Science" Blues

The regional historian travels poorly; a person with a graduate degree in American history and a thesis and museum experience centering, say, on New England, knows that taking a job in another part of the nation entails a loss of most or all of what he or she has learned. The region and its people are matters of little or no interest to new colleagues and audiences elsewhere. The exile, self-imposed though it may be, is real. By comparison art historians and scientists seem to have it easier; each is equipped to discuss artistic styles and natural laws the moment they step off the plane, whether in Albany, New York, or Albany, Georgia.

The regional historian is inherently disadvantaged. But a new job in a strange place should be a challenge and not be an excuse for soldiering. *The history museum director must be prepared to learn the history of his adopted region and the strengths and weaknesses of his museum's collections in that regard.* He may not have the stamina and determination to do this; if so, he should consider staying put. What seems to happen, since history personnel are usually compelled to move on at least once or twice in their careers, is for museum directors to bury themselves in administrative matters and claim to be too busy to learn about the materials in their care. How can one be a leader without setting an example? Accordingly, the history museum director should engage in historical study, narrow or limited in scope as it may of necessity be. The director who conducts hands-on tasks, and exposes them to public view, is better prepared to evaluate proposals and performance than the person whose bluff or uncertainty makes him comfortable only in his office and in venues far from home.

Let's for a moment look at history and art in terms of exhibits. The history exhibit is the most complex, and therefore the most problematic, of modalities; it is more cerebral and contrived and offers diverse avenues of interpretation. It is a potential minefield for perceived omissions and commissions of error; the history exhibit succeeds or fails on the strength of the conception and how it is fulfilled by the installation.

By comparison, the art exhibition is self-referring and is redeemable even when badly installed. Differences among exhibitions of art, history, and science have never been examined so far as the writer knows, even though practical understandings of constraints would ensue on what can and cannot be used as evidence—why, for example, a Winslow Homer painting is secondarily about boating or hunting for deer and trout, while a picture by Arthur Fitzwilliam Tait better illustrates these activities and so relieves the viewer of responsibility for anything other than identification.

These conditions inhere in the nature of the evidence itself; we cannot say more except to offer the following as cautionary advice. *The museum director should be sensitive to how history resists the universal formulations employed in art and science museums.* This is both the glory (history is choice) and the burden (history is inimitable) of historical interpretation.

## Exhibitions: The Locomotive That Pulls the Museum

History museums do many things, but the most public of their tasks, and the one for which they are held accountable by the lay person and professional alike, is the exhibition. Researchers may consult collections and the library, but special users like these are a small fraction of the number who will remember the museum chiefly through its exhibits. Low attendance, a small membership, visitors that are seen once but not again—these are symptoms of a low grade but chronic illness traceable to weak exhibits.

The problem is that exhibits are not changed often enough and are poorly conceived and presented. They may lack scope or reveal poor upkeep. Changing tastes leave permanent exhibits (an exception is the Ware Collection of glass models of plants and fruit by Leopold and Rudolph Blaschka at the Harvard Botanical Museum) marooned and irrelevant. The public can hardly be blamed for indifference if staff have long since passed through the galleries without taking notice of what is there. From this is inferred another rule: *The incoming director should examine exhibits and their surroundings while he or she still possesses a fresh, unbiased eye.* There are always moments of creative insight in a career spent at one institution, but special clarity seems greatest during early exposure to a new museum. The time for this is not long—probably the period married couples recall as their honeymoon.

The extent to which the director will be involved in the particulars of each exhibit will vary. But what the director cannot entirely delegate elsewhere is responsibility for assuring that the museum offers a balanced succession of exhibitions. Balance means weighing several factors critical to an exhibit program—temporary exhibits versus long term or "permanent" installations, the audience or audiences being addressed, and new knowledge or an issue to be examined or even commemorated. The museum itself, in a "new acquisitions" show, may constitute the subject. *The director should either request or assist in formulating a program of proposed exhibits for the next three to five years.* The schedule should reveal a museum that is striving to serve its community while satisfying those best qualified to judge the results, specialists and museum professionals.

The director will look at this plan and ask whether the proposals are consonant with the museum's statement of purpose. He should also ask whether the staff can deliver the goods. It is the director who must decide whether a course of action is worth the gains and losses that invariably accompany every worthwhile enterprise. Staff and trustees must be part of the decision-making process, after which they should then endorse the product, a plan. Consensus is necessary, but everyone, the director among them, must recognize that the buck stops with the director. *It is the director in whom the institution in its public dimensions is vouchsafed.*

The foregoing about exhibitions is derived largely from the writer's experiences at the Adirondack Museum, which utilizes extensive "permanent" installations in combination with changing displays. The museum tells of the history and culture of the people of the Adirondacks, both the residents and seasonal sojourners. Nature and climate still dominate this region of upstate New York, so much so that the museum in the last few years has been pondering how to sensitize visitors to a keener awareness of the link between what they see in the exhibits and what is around them in the outdoors—in the carpet of forest, mountains, and lakes stretching unbroken for sixty or more miles in any direction from Blue Mountain Lake. By late October, tourists have all but abandoned this remote wilderness, not to begin returning in numbers until the following May. Hence the museum is closed to the casual traveler during the winter season; in every respect save this, the museum offers the same services to members, school groups, and special users, such as researchers, on a year-round basis. The museum, which received 36 percent of its operating and capital budgets from a visitation of 100,433 in 1987, sees interpretive exhibits as central to the visitor's experience at the museum. Surveys show that the typical visit lasts nearly four hours and that a third of the visitors have been to the museum in a previous year, a good indication of satisfaction and loyalty from a constituency— the vacationing public—notably ungenerous with both.

New exhibits are partly intended to lure returnees. Some visitors can be expected to express disappointment when a 'permanent' exhibit is taken off view—they are sentimental favorites they mind missing. The museum's reply is that it cannot continue to add exhibits without removing old ones; and it says it hopes that favorites like sugaring and stoves will return in a fresh guise in a future year.

Is the Adirondack Museum's situation too special to be of use to other museums? Its setting is as rural as can be found in the northeast. In the third largest of New York's sixty-two counties, Hamilton County has a resident population of 5,000 and no stop light. The museum's seasonal cycle and tourist visitation are obvious distinctives, but these do not prevent history museums from doing what it has done. Its membership has grown from none to more than 1,800 in four years.

Let's look at a few aspects of exhibitions as they may apply to any history museum and its director.

**Alternating and finessing exhibits.** The Adirondack Museum alternates permanent and temporary exhibitions. Usually the long-term displays are historical and call for large outlays of time and money. Recent examples are the Mining Building (2,780 sq. ft.) and the Logging Building (5,184 sq. ft.), and their associated exhibits, and the Bull Cottage, an adaptive restoration and furnishing of a c. 1900 camp (2,275 sq. ft.). Changing exhibits usually mean loan exhibitions of art, such as the north country paintings of Frederic Remington and Adirondack watercolors by contemporary artist Allen Blagden, though there have been original single-season displays of historic maps and contemporary photographs. A catalog or book accompanies these original shows. Alternating long-term and temporary exhibits have allowed a small staff to sustain a heavy exhibition and construction program—hence the word "finesse" as used above.

**Art draws.** The Adirondack Museum benefits from the cachet of its paintings and loan exhibitions of art. More importantly, art reveals dimensions of expression and concepts not found in other holdings, which are practical or utilitarian, and it opens doors that have customarily been closed to history museums. Larger daily newspapers regularly cover openings at art museums, but history exhibits or openings do not seem to be newsworthy to judge by the scant attention paid to them.

**Exhibitions are agents of change.** Roughly half of the capital outlays at the Adirondack Museum have gone to exhibitions. The benefits are several. Besides the obvious one of gaining an addition, the museum has 1) obtained a new building or renovated an old one; 2) enhanced collections by donations of artifacts and by the transfer of things out of museum storage; 3) discarded outdated exhibitry and technology for replacements that are more durable and less labor-intensive (e.g., solid state message repeaters) or less greedy (low wattage gallery lights); 4) filled a gap in its knowledge about some aspect of the region's history; 5) garnered a new constituency for the museum; and 6) achieved economies in operating costs through retrofitting and other measures. The director can resolve some of the problems of an aging plant in the course of meeting his museum's interpretive responsibilities.

## Is There a Doctor in the House?

The museum director will seek outside help for projects likely to exceed the capacity of the staff to deliver. An entire project can be turned over to consultants, but this is expensive and will be resented if staff feel that strangers get the creative work while they must continue in the museum's equivalent of stoop labor. There is another objection—the packaged exhibition may charm and excite yet seem out of place, as though one found a Victorian chair in an Art Deco parlor. A consulting firm, especially one with a strong artistic head, may impose a *look* on an installation. The presence may exert a subtle influence when others try mounting exhibits elsewhere in the museum. Fortunately the director needn't choose simply between an exhibit done solely by staff or by a consultant.

Even the museum with a design capability may find new faces and approaches worth the cost. For its long-term exhibitions the Adirondack Museum undertakes research and scripting itself. For construction, de-

pending on the scope of the project, it usually relies on its own employees and on area contractors. The Adirondack Museum has never
had a full-fledged designer on staff, so it invites proposals from a consulting firm or perhaps a free-lance designer. A plan from the script is
roughed out and discussed. Once agreements have been reached following several visits back and forth, the working drawings are drawn up
and modified in what has been a continuing exchange between staff and
designer. Then the specifications for the exhibit are sent in a bid document to several firms that specialize in fabricating exhibits; conceivably
this could include the services of the firm for which the designer may
work. For reasons of control and fairness the Adirondack Museum has
kept designer and fabricator separate. Fabrication can include everything or just the fitments—dividers, pedestals, photographic enlarge-
ments, labels, and the like—that make an exhibit a finished, professional
product.

Control is important to the director, who should know that major
projects reach a point after which there is no return without grief. This
usually occurs when construction is well under way, at which point er-
rors or shortcomings are revealed and corrective steps are proposed
which will likely add to the final cost of the project. Such moments make
the hapless director vulnerable to being whipsawed by staff, consultant,
and contractor alike. Whatever he decides, the director, knowing that
the choice is likely to exact a price, must not act in haste, nor can he post-
pone a decision in the false hope the problem will somehow disappear.

The director without exhibit experience or savvy must necessarily
depend on others for information and advice. He should not be adver-
sarial, but he must insist that key players keep him informed of developments; if he can make a contribution, he should say so. Responsibility
will devolve to one member of the staff (other than the director), possibly the subject specialist or someone designed to coordinate the team of
players who produce the exhibit.

There should be a "paper trail" in which understandings or commit-
ments can be traced. Some people like doing business by telephone, but
this is an indulgence that can be risky when obligations are being assumed on behalf of the museum without follow-up. The rule to staff:
*Write it down, think out the consequences, share and clear it with others,
rewrite it. Exposition is a precondition to effective action.* Professional staff
must write coherently and be familiar with the computer and word
processor.

The operating costs of a proposed exhibit must be considered along
with those of planning and installation. This seems obvious, but there is
no motivation—unless it is required—for those submitting proposals to
volunteer information inimical to their chances of success. Watch

on-going expenses outside the museum's control; buildings and exhibits that are profligate users of energy can bring a museum to its knees. Questions the director should address include the following:

- Can this museum afford to pay upkeep costs for replacements and repairs?
- What about electricity, fuel oil, and gas for temperature, humidity and air controls, and for lighting?
- What of staffing, security, and housekeeping requirements?
- Will service contracts be called for?
- Should wear and tear on the fabric and mechanical system of the museum building be considered?

Consultants and even staff won't feel themselves obligated to raise questions like these, possibly on the assumption that they're the responsibility of someone else. That someone is the director.

## "Educational" and "Education" Not the Same

The history museum director should understand the difference between *educational* and *education*. Watching the replication of a 1787 fireworks display is not the same as mapping changing settlement patterns on the western frontier. *The director will try not to confuse education, which seeks specific outcomes, with the self-validating "educational."* Popular culture can be educational but its success derives from the belief that it is risk-free. Education entails risk. A society is in trouble that equates educational with education. Remember, however, that the appeal of the museum is that it affords choices while the classroom does not.

The museum educator will of necessity be drawn into theories about learning while the curator will not find them to be of much use. While the museum educator will not necessarily be a school teacher, this person must, if the museum has a school program worthy of the name, have some acquaintance with learning theories and know something of the realities of being a school teacher and student. *Aware that the educator is concerned with the process of learning as well as the content of learning, the director will not expect educators and curators to be interchangeable.*

Few directors understand education, in the museum or out of it, and most are happy as long as the educator does not bother him with problems about children and teachers. Still, students and teachers constitute the history museum's neediest audience. But despite decades of workshops, publications, funded research projects costing millions of dollars (who remembers Title III of the Elementary and Secondary Education Act?), and similar efforts aimed at fostering cooperation, each side—school and museum—waits for leadership from the other. There are museums and school districts where collaboration has been successful, in which both parties measurably benefit; but these are exceptions, triumphs of municipalities.

While policy supports the principle of state help to museums for their school offerings, as in New York State, this writer cannot think of any state legislature, including New York's, that appropriates money to museums through its state education department. Directors may be faulted for accepting the school program as a financial loss; and they perhaps should begin pressing their cause more forcibly than they've done. The indifference of superintendents and school boards may be a way of saying they see no reason to pay now when they've paid little or nothing in the past.

Future museum directors may find it necessary to reduce or withhold school services. Indeed, this may already be happening, albeit discreetly, without fanfare. The proliferation of museum offerings for adults since the late 1970s, undertaken without an equivalent expansion of programs for schools, can be seen as a preference by administrators for programs that favor adult audiences who can give the museum a better return on its investment.

The contents of these "educational" programs is limited only by one's imagination and nerve; field trips and travel are the most recent, but there are countless courses, of varying levels of intensity, as well. These offerings are not new—museums have been doing them for decades. What may be different is their packaging and aggressive marketing. The clientele and neighborhood of yore cannot sustain an institution's ambition to be a "national resource," which now is construed as license to fish for members and donors in the waters of other museums.

One wonders about the consequences of competition from within, as departments struggle to keep their place or establish it and find the task all-absorbing. And of competition from outside, as cultural institutions struggle for a place in the sun. Such pressures can be mitigated by dealing with the problem at its heart; cooperation that will assure each institution that it need participate only as long as it derives tangible benefits—increased visitation and income, and a membership happy at the prospect of being admitted to another museum at reduced cost. The Adirondack Museum and Shelburne Museum, which are separated by Lake Champlain, have reciprocated admission privileges for several years. Kindred museums in a region can exchange benefits and share in advertising and other forms of promotion at little or no cost or risk.

Here is the good news—history museums have a marketing advantage over their art and science counterparts. Each holds a variant mirror up to the American experience. This *particularity* of history museums, especially those oriented to distinctive ways of life, evokes positive responses from Americans and foreign travelers. History museum directors should take heed!

# 7

# The Director and the Research Function of Historical Institutions

by

Louis Leonard Tucker

LOUIS LEONARD TUCKER has been director of the Massachusetts Historical Society, Boston, since 1976. For the previous decade he served as State Historian of New York and Assistant Commissioner of Education in Albany. His career in historical administration commenced with the Cincinnati Historical Society where he was director from 1960 to 1966. Tucker received his B.A. (1952), M.A. (1954), and Ph.D. (1957) degrees from the University of Washington, and was a fellow at the Institute of Early American History and Culture (Williamsburg, Virginia) from 1958 to 1960. He is the author of numerous books, articles, and reviews in the field of American history and is a former president of AASLH.

The headquarters building of the Massachusetts Historical Society (1791), a private, independent institution located in Boston. It is the first historical society to be founded in the United States. Courtesy of the Massachusetts Historical Society, Boston, Massachusetts.

*T*he editor of this volume has asked me to focus on the topic, "The Director and the Research Function of Historical Institutions." He also requested me to touch upon these related issues:

1. How can the director foster the research use of his institution's collections on the part of outside (i.e., non-staff) scholars? In what way can the institution provide financial or other types of assistance or incentives for visiting scholars?
2. How can the director most effectively encourage the formation and/or further the contribution of a publications program that is consistent with his institution's mission and makes most productive use of his institution's collections?

The editor has also instructed me to draw upon pertinent illustrations from my professional experience—that is, to give the essay an autobiographical hue. I particularly welcome this approach for two reasons. Initially it has become obvious to me over the years that, just as no two snowflakes are exactly alike, so, too, are directors of historical institutions dissimilar. I have known every prominent historical administrator of the past quarter century, from the highly organized William T. Alderson, to the flamboyant Thomas Vaughan, and what I have been struck by is their marked individuality. No two directors bear similar characteristics, either in *management style* or personality. Heterogeneity is the hallmark of our group. What I am presenting, then, is a personal statement. I would not be so presumptuous as to represent myself as the *voice* of American historical administrators, with respect to the subject I have been requested to discuss. My colleagues and I have different points of view on this issue.

Secondly, just as directors differ, so, too, do historical institutions vary considerably. Indeed, their dissimilarities are so pronounced that they make one mindful of Heinz's celebrated 57 varieties of soup. My own town's historical society (Wellesley Historical Society, Massachusetts), which is essentially a house museum program, hardly bears comparison with such mammoth and multifarious institutions as the Ohio Historical Society or Colonial Williamsburg, or the society which I direct.

The size and character of a historical institution can often affect the managerial bent of a director. In some instances, the programmatic tradition of an institution is so deeply established that a director who goes against the grain of this tradition is courting disaster—i.e., a quick dismissal. I offer my own society as a case in point. If a director who was irrevocably committed to the philosophy of "popular history" sought to impose this type program upon the Massachusetts Historical Society (hereafter MHS), that person would have a brief tenure.

It may be proper, if not essential, to begin by sketching my professional background since my views on the role of research in historical administration have been profoundly influenced by the type of training I have received. At this writing (1990), I have been involved in historical administration for thirty years, all of them as a *chief executive officer.* My entrance into this field was an accident of fate. I had been trained as a colonial American historian at the University of Washington and was preparing for a lifelong career in the "halls of academe."

What needs to be underscored about my graduate training is the inordinate stress on research. As it has been for generations of graduate students of history, research was my "dram and drug." It suffused every aspect of this rigorous experience. I was conditioned never to accept any statement or source of information at face value. I was taught to apply the *rules of evidence,* and to examine an issue intensively before arriving at a conclusion. The climax of the graduate school regimen is the doctoral dissertation and the essence of this exercise is, of course, *research.* Little wonder, then, that research has been a principal desideratum in my value structure as a historical administrator.

In 1958, I was awarded a three-year, post-doctoral fellowship to the Institute of Early American History and Culture in Williamsburg, Virginia. The Institute, itself was a hot-bed of research. Every professional member of the staff was involved in a research project, either their own, or, in the case of editors, the work of external scholars. Research dominated the program.

Since Colonial Williamsburg was one of the two co-sponsors of the Institute and our offices were located in the heart of the restored area, I gained an insight into the workings of what is unquestionably America's largest, most heavily funded, and most efficiently managed outdoor history museum. (It was my first direct experience with a non-academic historical organization.) I learned that research represented the underpinning of that massive restoration. Every conceivable aspect of the program was linked with intensive research. For the Colonial Williamsburg staff, research was an article of faith. Nothing was done before the research had been completed.

When I was nearing the completion of my fellowship (1960), I received an offer "out of the blue" to become director of the Historical and Philosophical Society of Ohio[1] (hereafter HPSO), a small, regional historical society then located in the basement of the University of Cincinnati library. To that time I had never heard of the HPSO. I subsequently learned that it had been founded in 1822 and its program consisted of two elements—a library, and publications (a quarterly journal and an occasional monograph).

In presenting their offer, the officers of the society informed me of their plans to expand and vitalize all aspects of the program. Their intent was to "go public." A new building was part of this ambitious plan. They affirmed that they were committed to building "The Great Society" (in Cincinnati, that is).

After considerable soul-searching, I accepted their offer. I should note, parenthetically, that my entrance into historical administration reflected a significant trend that was taking place then, which has continued to this day. The historical agency field exploded during the early decades of the "Cold War." Existing programs experienced exponential growth and hundreds of new organizations sprang into being. Job opportunities for young historians with graduate degrees increased dramatically. Many began to enter this profession, bringing their distinctive values with them. For example, it is no accident that most of the larger and more reputable historical organizations of the United States are now headed by professional historians, and these institutions are noteworthy for the role that research plays in their various programs, from historic sites to museum exhibitions to publications. The influx of professional historians has markedly changed the character of these organizations.

Prior to the 1960s, only a handful of historians with advanced degrees were to be found in these institutions. The traditional habitat of this group had been the classroom. To paraphrase that old pejorative bromide about teachers, those historians with Ph.D.s who could, taught; those who could not, took employment with a historical organization.

I served as director of the HPSO for almost seven years, during which time we developed a spacious new building adjoining the Cincinnati Art Museum in beautiful Eden Park.[2] This new facility, and move to a more accessible site, marked the advent of a transformation of the society into a vibrant, high-visibility institution—which it has remained to this writing.

As director, I helped to institute a wide range of "popular history" programs in keeping with a mandate set forth by the board of trustees to broaden the society's outreach. Concurrently I sought to strengthen and improve the library, which, to me, was the heart of the institution. My personal convictions on the importance of research, plus my acquired knowledge of the Colonial Williamsburg operation, had led me to conclude that any programs we instituted, popular or scholarly, which were not based on exhaustive research, would lack substance and credibility. We thereupon increased the library staff, adding trained personnel, and embarked upon an accelerated cataloging effort. A number of collections had been in storage for years awaiting cataloging, and some of the society's major holdings had been processed inadequately by past untrained employees and volunteers. One of our principal objectives was to bring all of these collections under intellectual control.

We also began a number of other initiatives which were designed to increase the research use of the library by what I conceived to be its natural constituency, the graduate students and academic historians of southwest Ohio and neighboring northern Kentucky. We added academics to the governing board, and library and publications committees. We utilized them in organizing historical conferences and invited them to present lectures to our members. We importuned them to write articles in the HPSO's journal. In sum, the academic community became an integral part of the society's inner circle, and their value as researchers and teachers was brought to bear upon the total program, thereby providing it with a veneer of historical integrity and respectability. It is ironic to note that, for all the years the society was located on the University of Cincinnati campus, it had no active relationship with the historians of that institution who specialized in American history. This group, with one or two exceptions, manifested utter disdain for *local* history, regarding this field as beneath their professional dignity. I shared in this contempt since I was now a "historical society" historian. It is sad to report but I have encountered this type of intellectual arrogance in other settings as well. Academic historians have not been able to suffer our species gladly, notwithstanding our common origins.

From 1966 to 1976 I served as state historian of New York and assistant commissioner of Education (Albany, New York). This position embraced a wide range of responsibilities, from administering nearly thirty historic sites scattered about the state and the New York State Museum's history collection, to providing advice and technical services to over 700 historical societies and 1,100 local historians.

There is much that I could write about this ten-year experience in the context of the topic I have been assigned. Because of spatial constraints, I shall limit myself to but one issue. I witnessed a number of efforts to develop outdoor history museums in New York State during my stay there. Most, if not all, of these projects were inspired by civic boosters or entrepreneurs ("historical hucksters") who were motivated more by financial considerations than by their professed educational motives. In many cases, they had derived their inspiration from the Colonial Williamsburg program, which, they believed, was a resounding financial success.

What these neophytes never realized is that Colonial Williamsburg, like Rome, was "not built in a day"—nor was it as profitable an enterprise as they believed. The colonial capital was restored over a number of years (this process continues even to this day), and was based, as noted earlier, upon prodigious, painstaking research. Behind every structure, public program, or specific exhibit was a mountain of research. The enormous scope of this research effort came as a revelation to me during my residence there. I was awed by it.

I was also awed by its Olympian cost. The Colonial Williamsburg research staff, which was divided into three basic units (historical, architectural, and archaeological) was a sizable contingent of well-trained professionals. Their standards were as high as their cost.

This factor was either unknown to the boosters and entrepreneurs of New York State or they failed to comprehend its financial implications. The message I constantly conveyed to these groups, and it was never received with glee, was that, unless they were willing to commit millions of dollars to research, they had better abandon their plans to replicate a Colonial Williamsburg-type program. And, if they insisted upon developing their project on a base of superficial research, they were doomed to failure. Was my advice accepted? In most cases, it was—grudgingly. On two occasions, it was not heeded. Those projects subsequently failed.

In 1977, I was appointed director of the Massachusetts Historical Society. First, a few words about this extraordinary institution. The MHS was the first historical society founded in the United States (1791). It is a private, independent institution. Contrary to popular belief, it is not an agency of the Commonwealth of Massachusetts.

The history of the MHS can be divided into two distinct epochs. From its founding to the period of World War I, it functioned largely as an all-male, private cultural club. Its library, which was well-stocked with manuscripts, books and pamphlets, was used almost exclusively by the members, a small body (less than one hundred) of patrician-historians from the Greater Boston area. A number of these men were the leading literary and intellectual figures of the nation (examples: Ralph Waldo Emerson, Henry Wadsworth Longfellow, George Bancroft, Edward Everett, Francis Parkman, William Hickling Prescott, and John L. Motley).

In addition to administering a library, the MHS sponsored a publication program, producing over the years a significant series of documentary works and monographs. These were distributed to historical societies and other cultural and educational institutions in the United States and Great Britain. Publications represented the only form of outreach by the Society at that time. They linked the MHS with the scholarly world at large.

While "amateurs," the men of the MHS were competent historians, adhering to strict scholarly standards. They prided themselves on the high quality of their research and felicitous literary style. They were an unusually gifted group.

With the advent of graduate historical instruction in the early twentieth century, the MHS entered a second phase of institutional development. While retaining its policy of elective membership, the MHS permitted greater access to its library by non-members. The club-like atmosphere began to disappear and the MHS began to assume the character of a modern research library. By the 1930s, it had become, for all intent and purpose, an "open" society. A growing number of graduate students and scholars traveled to Boston to use its incomparable resources (at no charge). This transformation led to the development of a paid, professional staff of librarians, historians, and editors; previously, members had administered these programs as unpaid volunteers. The MHS hired its first director in 1940. At this writing, there are twenty-seven full-time employees, the bulk of whom are trained personnel. In sum, it is a highly professional staff.

While many significant changes have taken place in the MHS in the past two centuries, its basic program and mission have remained surprisingly constant. The main components of its program are now as they were in the first years: a library and scholarly publications. The same is true of its mission, which is to collect and preserve historical sources and disseminate historical information. Research was of transcendent importance at the founding and remains so today. What needs to be emphasized is that the MHS has always been a center of "serious research." It has never made "popular history" its main bill of fare. While a "historical society" in name, it is really classified as an "independent research library."[3]

There have been only four directors in the past half century (including the incumbent) and all were strong advocates of historical research and engaged in facilitating this activity. None had to force the concept of research upon the MHS. Quite the contrary, this tradition or principle has been deeply ingrained in the institutional marrow of the MHS.

My own experience as a stimulator of scholarship at the MHS represents continuity of a tradition, no innovation. (Since this effort is really a collaborative enterprise and involves others, namely our librarian and editor of publications, I prefer to use *we* hereafter rather than *I*.)

In keeping with tradition, we *advertise* our holdings at every available opportunity in an effort to attract researchers. We are especially active when we have new *wares* for our constituents—i.e., a heretofore unused collection of source materials. The Caroline Healy Dall Papers is a relevant example.

Here is a bit of essential background on Dall. She was a leading reformer and essayist in her time (1811–1917). A writer, lecturer, and teacher, Dall was active in the women's suffrage and anti-slavery movements, and the underground railroad. She was also a Unitarian activist, and the founder of the Social Science Association. She carried on a brisk correspondence with a number of leading historical figures of her era (e.g., Louisa May Alcott, Margaret Fuller, Susan B. Anthony, William Lloyd Garrison, Theodore Parker, Elizabeth Cady Stanton, Charles Sumner, and Wendell Phillips).

As she neared the end of her life, Dall came to recognize the research value of her private papers, which were stored in three large trunks. She offered these materials to the MHS in 1900 and they were accepted grudgingly. Robert C. Winthrop, a prominent member of the society and soon to be its president, was one of the opposers of the gift. He was afflicted with the conventional sexist bias of his generation. As he wrote to President Charles Francis Adams II, on March 18, 1900:

> I observed in yesterday's Transcript that our excellent friend S.A.G. had just celebrated his 70th birthday. The much needed weeding of printed matter belonging to the M.H.S. should thus seem appreciably nearer, tho' you and I may not live to witness it. Indeed, I incline to think rubbish on the increase.
>
> When my father moved from Summer Street to Pemberton Square (now more than half a century ago) he found his next door neighbor to be an unattractive old party named Mark Healey, whose daughter Caroline had married a Unitarian minister named Dall and was then, and for long afterward, an authoress in a small way, with an ambition to regenerate her sex, combined with a propensity to "interview" men of note. Availing herself of her propinquity, she from time to time plied my father with all sorts of questions and at great length, causing him to exclaim "That lady's name ought not be Dall, but Dull." Imagine my surprise to discover, on p. 310 of the recently issued Serial, that last November the Society accepted the following gift from this now venerable person:—"Three trunks containing type-written material: seven quarto volumes of MSS, 12 printed volumes, 5 pamphlets, and three other volumes of MSS," *the whole apparently autobiographical!*
>
> No wonder the new building is already too small for our purposes, and the joke of the matter is that as I hear whispered, the lady had vainly offered this cumbrous material to other institutions, who respectfully declined to house it.

For many years, Dall's three trunks lay at rest in the society's stacks alongside other uncataloged collections, not an uncommon experience in major research libraries. They were "discovered" when the women's rights movement blossomed in the 1960s and quickly assumed a top-priority status. Our staff cataloged and microfilmed them and developed a guide to the collection. They were not available to researchers for inspection.

Our next step was to publicize this significant resource and alert scholars across the nation to its availability. To this end we entered the collection into OCLC, the national cataloging network. In our frequent informal contact with visiting and local scholars, we provided information on these papers. We featured segments of the collection in exhibitions in the MHS. We fully briefed our sister institution in Cambridge, Radcliffe College's Schlesinger Library, which specializes in the study of women's history. This library had acquired a small portion of Dall's papers and we arranged to have these microfilmed and added to the general collection.

Because of this cumulative effort to *spread the word,* the Dall Papers has become one of the most heavily used collections in the library. This research is already bearing fruit. With each passing year, we are noticing more references to this collection in articles in scholarly journals. Some doctoral dissertations and monographs relating to Dall are currently being developed. One scholar is currently preparing select portions of her journal for publication. In short, scholarly attention to Dall is at a high level. Her "rubbish" has become a researcher's *El Dorado.*

Some of our manuscript collections are so well known to scholars that they do not require a heavily mounted campaign of publicity and special pleading to increase their usage (e.g., the Adams, Jefferson, Winthrop, Lodge, Revere, Parkman, Knox, and Saltonstall Papers). Nonetheless, we do call attention to these holdings as a matter of general policy when we discuss the research potential of our materials with scholars or other prospective users. This type of *salesmanship* is considered part of our professional responsibility as stewards of these historic holdings.

Another technique we have utilized to advantage to publicize our holdings to prospective users is to print articles in our *Proceedings* on a given theme in which we delineate the society's resources (principally primary) on this subject. Since the *Proceedings* is primarily intended for scholars, it is a proper vehicle for transmitting this type of biographical information. To date, we have published articles on "The Old China Trade," "Unitarianism," and "Universalism." In preparation are articles on "Quakers and Baptists," "Episcopalians," and "The Civil War." Our long-range objective is to publish articles on a wide range of subjects for which our holdings are of high quality and, when this series has been completed, incorporate all of the essays into one volume. This work should be an invaluable reference tool for scholars.

The MHS is blessed with a large and significant portrait collection. One observer has described it as a "national treasure." Consisting of more than three hundred paintings, it contains examples by most of the major artists in the history of American portraiture (e.g., John Smibert, Joseph Blackburn, Joseph Badger, John Singleton Copley, John Trumbull, Gilbert Stuart, and Chester Harding). Their subjects are equally important in American life (e.g., Increase Mather, Samuel Sewell, Thomas Hutchinson, Peter Faneuil, George Washington, John Hancock, the Marquis de Lafayette, and Daniel Webster).

From its founding, the MHS has not been an active collector of paintings. It acquired these items as an afterthought, usually when families donated manuscripts, books, and other paper sources. The art works represented an incidental gratuity. The MHS traditionally regarded these items as artifacts for display, not research materials.

The MHS printed listings of its art works in 1838, 1885, and 1949, but these were skimpy in content and of only slight value to researchers. They lacked illustrations and detailed provenance notes. In truth there was little interest in our art works until the mid-twentieth century.

As in the case of the Dall Papers, the portraits were *discovered* in recent years when public and scholarly interest in early American art works began to increase. They came to be recognized as a major research resource, not a tangential asset.

In the 1970s, we concluded that the MHS had an obligation to bring this collection to the attention of art historians and other serious researchers. We began laying plans for a printed catalog of our portraits. The effort finally came to fruition in 1988 with the publication of *Portraits in the Massachusetts Historical Society.* This book has been received with joy and gratitude by art historians in particular. They instantly recognized its value. As John Wilmerding, former deputy director of the National Gallery of Art and one of the leading authorities on American art, wrote in the foreword:

> The collection of portraits documented here in their entirety for the first time provides a vivid index of the cultural identity and aspirations respectively of Boston, Massachusetts, and America. Aside from including images of some of our nation's most famous figures by many of our greatest artists, this group of often stern and worthy faces tells much about Boston's role as a first seat of learning and culture in the New World. Additionally, their lives and circumstances illuminate the powerful political traditions shaped by Massachusetts minds but extended to the other colonies and ultimately to the republic at large. More broadly, these collective presences inform us about our early and ongoing sense of confidence, ambition, self-reliance, and individual achievement.

Curators of museums have also expressed positive statements about the catalog, for obvious reasons. They are constantly on the alert for paintings to borrow for exhibitions. The MHS has welcomed their interest since it has had a generous lending policy in the past half century.

Since the publication of the portrait catalog, we have begun to notice an increase in loan requests.

Another technique we have employed to stimulate research in our collections is to sponsor orientation sessions for faculty members of Boston-area universities, which offer graduate courses in American history and related fields (e.g., political science, American material culture). We provide these instructors with an intensive briefing on the sources and discuss the range of possibilities for research topics. We also show examples of sources from our collections.

On occasion, we invite a particular instructor and his or her students to the MHS and present a similar briefing, coupled with an orientation on the various card catalogs and finding aids in the library.

With respect to the ways a director can provide financial or other types of assistance or incentives for visiting scholars, I can only comment on what our policies are at the MHS. The conventional form of financial assistance is the research fellowship and we do provide such support. Using income from endowed funds and special grants, we have been able to offer from twelve to sixteen short-term fellowships annually in recent years. These are competitive fellowships.

Furthermore, it is a long-standing tradition of the MHS to provide "tender loving care" to all visiting researchers, particularly graduate students who need special attention because of their weak financial situation and lack of experience in research libraries. As hundred of prefaces in doctoral dissertations and published monographs will attest, the MHS has a reputation as an hospitable institution and researcher's paradise.

This director vividly recalls conducting research on his doctoral dissertation in the MHS in 1956 and being greeted warmly by Director Stephen T. Riley and taken to an elegant French restaurant for lunch. At no other research library in the United States or Great Britain did I receive such gracious hospitality and solicitous service as I did at the MHS.

Long-term researchers are made to feel *at home.* They are invited to attend all MHS functions, from lectures to the annual Spring Reception to holiday office parties. They are permitted to use the staff kitchen and lounge for coffee breaks and lunch. Every Thursday they are encouraged to join senior staff members at a dutch-treat lunch in nearby restaurants. In sum, they are regarded as part of *the family.*

The director of the MHS does not have to make any special effort to encourage the formation and/or further the continuation of its publications program—it is consistent with the society's mission and makes the most productive use of its collections. From its birth in 1791 the MHS has been committed fiercely to a publications program. This was one of the main reasons for its founding. It lay at the heart of the MHS's dual mission of preserving sources and disseminating historical information.

What better way to accomplish both objectives than by publishing the documents the MHS was collecting? So reasoned Jeremy Belknap, the founder. He would "multiply the copies," thereby assuring the preservation of information and he would help to educate the citizenry about American history and, simultaneously, promote public virtue and patriotism, the ultimate mission of the MHS. And so Belknap began to publish documents in a newly established newspaper, the *American Apollo* (as a supplement) in 1792 and, in the same year, produced the first volume of the society's unparalleled *Collections* series.

So it began. What Belknap established, later generations carried forward. *Collections, Proceedings,* Sibley's *Biographical Sketches of Harvard Graduates, Photostat Americana, Journals of the House of Representatives*—it is safe to say that the MHS has published more high-quality historical works, both documentary and monographic, than any other historical institution in the United States. These publications are known in particular to every scholar of early American history, and taken *in toto,* constitute a veritable *vade mecum* of the history of the nation.

Research is a *sine qua non* at the MHS. It is the major foundation stone of the institution. Scholars come from far and wide to conduct research in the library. When not servicing these scholars, our library staff is engaged in its own research chores; cataloging manuscripts, broadsides, prints, maps, and even coins and medals. Members of the publications staff pursue research on the MHS works in preparation, from the Adams Papers to the *Proceedings* to special monographs. A number of retired staff members, who are provided offices and other forms of support, also engage in research projects, some pertaining to MHS-sponsored works, others relating to their personal interests. One retiree is readying for publication a two-volume edition of Robert Treat Paine's personal and business correspondence. Another is editing a volume of the Winthrop Family Papers. A third is editing a volume of the Saltonstall Family Papers.

As director, I encourage our professional staff to participate in scholarly research with publication as the objective. We permit these employees to spend a portion of their work schedule on either personal projects or MHS–sponsored publications. This practice extends even to the director. After three or four years of intermittent research, sandwiched between administrative duties, I published a book in 1990 on the founding of the MHS. Currently, I am conducting research on a bicentennial history of the MHS and preparing an extended essay for the printed catalog of the MHS treasures that will be exhibited at the Boston Museum of Fine Arts in 1991.

This is the MHS way. Is it relevant to other historical institutions?

Probably not. The MHS has a distinctive history and character. It is a "peculiar institution." Research is, and always has been, its *raison d'etre*. Given my training and background, this director would not have it any other way.

# 8

# The Director as Legal Guardian

by

William T. Alderson

WILLIAM T. ALDERSON has spent a distinguished career in the service of American museums, most notably those in the field of history. In 1990 he retired as president of Old Salem, Inc., in Winston-Salem, North Carolina, prior to which he was director of the Strong Museum, Rochester, New York, and the Museum Studies Program and the Winterthur Program in the Conservation of Historic and Artistic Objects at the University of Delaware. From 1964 to 1978 he was director of AASLH following twelve years with the Tennessee State Library and Archives, the last three as its director. He has a B.A. from Colgate University and M.A. and Ph.D. degrees in history from Vanderbilt University. Alderson has published extensively in the field of state and local history. Over the years he has been strongly committed to professional organizations, serving on the Council and the Executive Committee of AAM, as the first chair of the AAM Accreditation Commission, and in a variety of other capacities. He has received special awards from several professional groups in recognition of his many contributions to the museum field.

William T. Alderson, the retired president of Old Salem, Inc., with resource materials illustrating the dichotomy between the concentration of responsibility and interest of yesterday's museum director and today's. Courtesy of Old Salem Restorations, Winston-Salem, North Carolina.

*O*nce upon a time, and not so very long ago, historical societies and museums didn't have to be very concerned about legal issues. Neither, for that matter, did most nonprofit organizations. We were seldom sued because, after all, we were engaged in noble work in behalf of a grateful public, with much of the labor coming from dedicated volunteers. We were supposed to have an exemption letter from the Internal Revenue Service in order for our donors to get tax deductions, but if we had failed to get one, it was possible to get it retroactively. We didn't have to classify our employees as exempt or nonexempt or pay time-and-a-half for overtime, because we weren't subject to the Fair Labor Standards Act; and our participation in the Social Security program was optional. And, of course, OSHA, ERISA, COBRA, and other now-familiar acronyms weren't yet even gleams in some congressman's eye.

Today, of course, we are beset in every direction by legal requirements and potential liability. We share with ordinary mortals the joys of being full participants in a litigious society. We spend money we would rather have go to programs to purchase director and officer liability insurance, or else live nervously in the hope that the indemnification clause in our bylaws won't be called into play. We pay substantial legal fees to be sure that what we do is not in conflict with the latest laws or regulations. The newest history book stays on the shelf while we grope our way through bureaucratic and legal jargon to be sure we understand what is required of our institutions. For along with all the other things demanded of directors, we bear the principal responsibility for keeping our institutions out of legal trouble.

For most of us, this is not an easy burden. Few of us are trained in the law, but somehow we must learn enough about the law to do three things. First, we must be sufficiently aware of the laws and regulations governing our institutions to be in compliance. Second, we must somehow develop the ability to spot potential legal entanglements before they can occur. And third, we must develop the good judgment to know when we ought to consult an attorney and when it is reasonably safe to make a decision based on our own knowledge of the law. How do we accomplish this?

In my opinion the very best way is to attend the "ALI-ABA Course of Study, Legal Problems of Museum Administration." The first course was offered in 1973 by the American Law Institute–American Bar Association, cosponsored by the Smithsonian Institution and the American Association of Museums. It has been held annually ever since, with a new curriculum each year. It is invaluable for an understanding of recent changes in the law and for discussion of current applications of existing laws. Registrants are a mix of museum professionals and lawyers, and instruction is geared to nonlawyers. A five- to six-hundred-page study manual containing outlines of each presentation is issued every year to each registrant, and additional copies are available from ALI-ABA. I have attended most of the courses. They have consistently been outstanding educational experiences, and I frequently refer to back issues of the study manual. I have also found that attending the course and having the study manual have enabled me to pass new information and citations along to the attorneys for my museum, which has saved them research time and thus reduced my museum's legal bills.

For those who cannot attend ALI-ABA there are useful publications that will be of some help. Marie C. Malaro's *A Legal Primer on Managing Museum Collections* (Washington: Smithsonian Institution Press, 1985) is broader in scope than the title indicates and is the best single-volume legal treatment of the field currently available. Stephen E. Weil's *Beauty and the Beasts: On Museums, Art, the Law, and the Market* (Washington: Smithsonian Institution Press, 1983) is an excellent collection of essays by one of the most thoughtful and articulate writers in the museum field, a lawyer as well as a museum administrator. Marilyn Phelan's *Museums and the Law* (Nashville: American Association for State and Local History, 1982) is a useful one-volume reference with considerable attention to tax law and, therefore, in need of revision to cover the extensive changes since its publication. My own office would not be complete without a thousand page book by Howard Oleck titled *Non-profit Corporations, Organizations, and Associations* (5th ed., Englewood Cliffs, NJ: Prentice-Hall, 1988). This is a very useful reference book covering everything from how to create a nonprofit to how to dissolve it, and lots of information on how it should be run to meet legal requirements. It is now dated, but still worth having.

The spotting of potential legal entanglements will certainly be helped by ALI-ABA and by these books, but the legal field is changing constantly as new laws are passed or new regulations or rulings issued, and one needs a way to keep up with the changes. *History News, Museum News*, and the newsletters of AASLH, AAM, and the AAM regional conferences are obvious sources. *Nonprofit World*, published by the Society for Nonprofit Organizations, deals with legal issues on a regular basis, as does *The NonProfit Times*, a newer magazine published by the Davis Information Group. *The Kiplinger Washington Letter* and *The Kiplinger Tax Letter* provide excellent and succinct information on new legislation and government regulations. There are also newsletters issued by some of the larger accounting firms and law firms for their clients, which have the added advantage of providing information about both federal law and state and local issues.

Out of all this reading, and perhaps attendance at an ALI-ABA program, you should have developed an awareness of the legal components of your work as director and enough knowledge to feel comfortable making some legal decisions yourself. You will doubtless have searched out your organization's articles of incorporation and either verified that you are carrying out your chartered purposes, or that revisions are needed to come into compliance. You will have studied your organization's bylaws and, again, determined that the organization is complying with the bylaws; and you will also have realized that failure to comply could invalidate actions taken by the board. You will have located your Tax Exempt Determination Letter that the Internal Revenue Service issued years ago and you will have checked to make sure the proper tax forms are being filed.

You will also have begun to examine your shop merchandise with a new eye, wondering whether it is "related" to your chartered purposes or might be subject to Unrelated Business Income Tax (UBIT). You will have looked into the requirements of the Employee Retirement Income Security Act (ERISA) to see whether your retirement plan conforms to legal requirements and whether it is "nondiscriminatory" (this will probably require help from your insurance carrier or your attorney). You will have gotten from the Department of Labor copies of the applicable provisions of the Fair Labor Standards Act, and if it applies to your institution, you will have determined which employees are affected by it and which are exempt, and what kinds of records you will need to prove you have complied. And you will have studied the regulations of the Equal Employment Opportunity Commission to see whether you are in compliance and will also have determined whether your institution is required, in addition, to have an Affirmative Action plan.

These are all federal law and regulations, and you can probably take the necessary steps yourself. But be forewarned that compliance with the laws of your state, county, or municipality is also required, and those laws may be even stricter. For that reason it would be well to consult legal counsel from time to time on your steps to comply with federal law and make sure that nothing additional is required to meet local requirements.

In deciding whether to consult an attorney, you need to recognize that some of your decisions subject your museum or historical society to only minor risk, while others expose the institution to very high risk if not done correctly. For example there are severe penalties for failure to comply with the provisions of ERISA, especially if, even unwittingly, your plan can be found to be discriminatory in favor of your professional and higher paid staff. In general, the higher the risk the more the likelihood that you should consult an attorney.

There are also some actions your institution takes that should more or less routinely cause you to seek legal advice. For example I would not enter into a formal contract that had not been drawn up or at least approved by our own attorney; and I would not enter into a letter of agreement, such as a letter offering employment, without having learned from a lawyer what is safe to say and what is potential future trouble. Real estate transactions need legal review by your attorney, as do legal matters involving taxes.

An area where, in today's society, careful legal counseling is most needed is the relationship of your institution to its personnel. This begins with your personnel manual, which if not properly written can be construed to be an employment contract. Have it carefully reviewed before issuing it; your attorney can save you untold future trouble. I usually consult an attorney before dismissing an employee, if I think there is any possibility of a lawsuit, and I have learned that one is well advised to have a "paper trail" documenting unsatisfactory performance. I have also learned that supervisors who charitably give higher ratings than are deserved in the annual performance appraisal ultimately may be victimized by having to put up with an unsatisfactory employee for whom there are no reasonable grounds for dismissal. Sound legal advice can help us avoid such situations, and whether or not we approve of our litigious state of existence, we owe it to our institution to protect it from harm.

Given, then, that we need legal advice from time to time, how ought we to go about getting it? Only a very few museums in the United States need or can afford their own legal staff. Most large institutions have a law firm that does all or most of their legal work. Sometimes the firm works on an annual retainer to cover up to a specified number of hours of work. More often the work is simply billed at the charge per hour of the attorney who does the work, with the charges of senior partners much more than for beginning associates or interns. Some organizations regard large law firms as too expensive and seek out a small law office or even try to arrange *pro bono* legal advice by electing a lawyer to the board of trustees.

Such arrangements may work satisfactorily where the degree of risk is modest, but my own preference, growing out of work with several large institutions, is for a law firm big enough to have specialists in the fields common to nonprofit organizations: labor law, tax law, contracts, estates and trusts, real estate, and liability. Having once paid a heavy price for the mishandling of what seemed a simple legal matter by an attorney whose principal work was in a different field of law, I prefer having a specialist to handle my legal work. The big law firms are more likely to have the specialist you need, and while the fees may be a bit higher, it shouldn't take the specialist as long to come up with the answer you need. You may also be lucky enough, as I have been, to find a big law firm that is willing to reduce its fees for a nonprofit historical organization.

Whatever the choice of legal advice, the really important point is that the director of the organization must recognize that, along with all of his or her other duties, there is a responsibility to see that the organization runs in compliance with an increasing body of regulations imposed by federal, state, and local governments, and that it conducts its affairs in a manner that avoids the expense—and the bad publicity—of being involved in lawsuits that might have been avoided. Much as we might prefer to spend our time studying history and our collections, when we become directors our primary duty is stewardship for an institution that serves the people of today and generations yet unborn. That stewardship includes being a guardian for the legal affairs of our organization, sometimes doing the job ourselves, sometimes retaining the expertise of legal specialists, and along the way developing the judgment to make the correct choice.

# 9

# The Director as Organizer and Energizer for Planning

by

Bryant F. Tolles, Jr.

BRYANT F. TOLLES, JR., is director of the Museum Studies Program and associate professor of history and art history at the University of Delaware. From 1974 to 1984 he served as director of the Essex Institute, Salem, Massachusetts, prior to which time he was assistant director of the New Hampshire Historical Society. He has a Ph.D. in history from Boston University and M.A.T. (history) and B.A. (American studies) degrees from Yale University. He is chair of the Committee on Museum Professional Training, a member of the Council, and a senior examiner for the Accreditation Commission of the American Association of Museums and is also active in AASLH and regional museum organizations. He has served as a consultant for historical societies and museums and has published books, articles, and reviews in the fields of museology and American architectural and social/cultural history.

An artist's conception of the proposed Essex Institute Museum Neighborhood, where a coordinated program of restoration, renovation, and interpretation will result in a historic world on one city block in downtown Salem. The project is the outgrowth of master planning which commenced in the early eighties, and culminated in an NEH-funded planning study completed in 1984. Courtesy of the Essex Institute, Salem, Massachusetts.

*P*icture, if you will, the proverbial image of a disabled ship drifting rudderless in a stormy sea, helpless in the face of uncertain elements, with little or no control over where it is going, and how it is going to get there. With the inability to chart its future direction and to generate the resources to make headway, this ship will experience a very unsettling if not disastrous voyage. Only an accident of good fortune will enable it to right its course and achieve its ultimate goal—safe arrival at its final destination, its crew, passengers, and cargo intact. Only then will its captain be able to assess the circumstances and implications of this risky adventure and ponder ways to ensure that his ship steer a straighter, less perilous, and incident-free course on future voyages.

By way of analogy consider next a museum proceeding aimlessly from year to year, decade to decade, without benefit of planning—that vital steering mechanism without which no institution can fulfill its mission in a progressive, rational fashion. Like the captain of our mythical ship at sea, the director of this museum can expect confusing and trying times in the absence of the means to guide his institution on a prescribed course. Presented with such circumstances this museum will surely founder, failing to set and achieve goals and objectives, and inefficiently utilizing its resources.

Without a full commitment to planning as a regularized, high priority function, museums of all kinds, including those in the history field, stand little chance of realizing success as meaningful, contributing educational entities. Plainly and simply, as the above parallel scenarios should demonstrate, planning is an activity in which all museums must routinely engage to guarantee future survival. Many in the museum field think that planning is the single most important management function, to which all others should be considered secondary and from which all others emanate. I share this conviction. No director should be without it! No director should fail in his duty to assure that it happens recurrently at his own institution! All directors, whether at museums large or small, possess the authority, the opportunity, and the obligation, as embodied in most CEO job descriptions, to organize and energize the planning process.

## Planning: What It Is and Why Museums Need It

Over the years planning has been variously defined by people representing many different fields. In fact so many definitions of planning have been put forth that it is very difficult to arrive at one that satisfactorily incorporates its essence, its many facets, and its end product. To some it is a mystifying, almost intimidating process, while to others it is comfortable, reassuring, and patently obvious. For its inspiration and organizational framework the museum world has looked to the profit sector and the academic realm, where, in both instances, the record of planning has far deeper roots. Fortunately, on the strength of this sound legacy, the image of what planning is within the museum context has in recent years become increasingly well defined. As a systematic process in museums, though, it is still a relatively new phenomenon; but we are fast learning from experience and gaining a better sense of what it consists and what its benefits are.

*The American Heritage Dictionary*, to which one may refer for a current general definition, defines planning as that organized activity which results in "a detailed scheme, program, or method worked out . . . for the accomplishment of an object."[1] This definition, concise and hard to quibble with, certainly is applicable to the nonprofit sector and specifically museums. Planning should also be viewed as a process that is inherently continual. A recent *History News* article describes it as "really nothing more than the management of change."[2] Through planning, institutions set long-range and short-term goals, formulate ways to attain these goals, and assess the results. Management guru Peter Drucker perhaps best defines planning as "decision-making with an eye to the future."[3] In the most elementary terms it is a process that answers the following questions about an institution: What is it and what is its purpose? Why was it established? Where has it been? Where is it now? Where does it wish to go in the future? How is it going to get there? How is it going to evaluate its progress along the way?

## Recently Published Perspectives on the Planning Process

During the 1970s and 1980s there has been a plethora of material published treating both profit and nonprofit sector planning in the United States. Some of this literature has been outstanding, while some has added very little to our understanding of the subject. Some has been theoretical, and some has been more methodological and prescriptive. Until the last few years, those associated with museums seeking to expand their knowledge about planning had no option other than to wade through the many books, manuals, and articles treating the profit sector, there being virtually no useful literature specifically directed toward planning for museums. Fortunately, this oversight has recently been resolved, largely as a result of publications generated through the auspices of the American Association of Museums, the American Association for State and Local History, the Canadian Museums Association, and other publishers.

A cursory review of some of the most significant of these writings is called for before proceeding to a more comprehensive discussion of planning and the role of the director in that process. One of the best general overviews for museums is a 1982 *History News* article, "Thinking

Ahead," by George E. Hicks[4] in which the author defines long-range planning, identifies its key ingredients, and outlines its benefits. A 1982 *Museum News* piece, "Preparing a Blueprint for Tomorrow" by Larry Ter Molen,[5] discusses long-range planning as it relates to museum development and marketing. A manual-style collection of essays under the title *Planning Our Museums* was sponsored in 1983 by the National Museums of Canada, and though it deals largely with planning for new construction and renovation, it does not neglect overriding precepts, the human element, and processes of implementation.[6]

In a 1985 essay in *Museum News* lawyer and museum administrator Peter J. Ames comments extensively about a process only tangentially related to but still important for long-range planning—"institutional renewal or mission-driven strategic planning."[7] Two excellent articles, published in *History News* and *Museum News* in 1983 and 1985 by former Virginia museum and historic site consultant, the late Suzanne Schell,[8] treat the concept, process, and results of institutional self-study as one of the essential components of planning. Strategic planning (to be defined below), another of the major phases of the total institutional planning process, is considered in some depth and with considerable sophistication by Alice McHugh and Robert Simerly in 1980 and 1982 articles appearing in *Museum News*.[9]

But probably the best and most useful discussion of planning for museums, certainly for those in the field of history, is contained in the essay "Institutional Master Planning for Historical Organizations and Museums" published by AASLH's Technical Information Service in 1985 as *Technical Report* 11, researched and coauthored by museum consultant Hedy A. Hartman and Suzanne Schell. Given the existence of this very thorough and for the most part extremely enlightened document, and my general agreement with its content, it would be redundant for me to describe in excessive detail what would be essentially the same or even similar rationale for and process of planning. There is no particular purpose served by attempting to "reinvent the wheel." I must further point out, though, that neither in this essay nor in any other recent work published in this country or Canada has the planning role of the director, in large as well as small history museum situations, been broadly and critically considered. But it is pertinent as well as convenient to cite and review the Hartman and Schell recommended institutional planning process as a model from which one may develop a discussion of the directorial role. This I will do in the balance of this essay.

Before proceeding on, however, I must draw your attention to one important caveat—while there may be many outstanding models to emulate, every institution should go about planning in a manner tailored to its own philosophy, people, resources, and modus operandi. What is one institution's pleasure could very easily be another's anathema.

## Structuring the Planning Process

It is difficult for anyone ever associated with top level administration in the history museum field to argue with Hartman's and Schell's opening point that "the institutional planning process is essential for the most effective management of historical institutions." The entire planning process is calculated to produce future guidelines for an institution through a broad-sweeping critical review, the definition of suitable goals and objectives, and the development of the means to achieve them. As Hartman and Schell point out, "institutional planning should begin with a self-study and result in a long-range plan." The self-study or assessment (I prefer to call it "critical review") phase is intended to analyze the current status, operations, and programs of an institution, while its sequel, the long-range plan, "details future institutional directions, resulting in a single document for the organization." Only in this way can an institution's mission be effectively satisfied and regularly examined in order to ensure the most expeditious delivery of programs and services.

In the Hartman/Schell model the planning process (which they identify under the general heading of "master planning") is divided into three distinct but intimately related phases: "assessment or self-study, institutional goal setting, and strategic institutional planning." During the self-study phase a special planning committee is entrusted with both the systematic review of past and present programs and operational practices of the institution and with identification of its strengths and weaknesses. The results of such an assessment are "then reflected upon by the planning team to set goals and objectives for the institution over three to five years." The third or strategic planning phase then follows, charting "very specifically how the staff and trustees will implement the goals and objectives."[10] By adopting this approach to master planning, institutions large as well as small, develop the capability to control their own future destinies in a logical, organized, and visionary manner. It will usually, however, take them three months to a year to do so, and will necessitate continual updating over future years.

## The Self-Study or Critical Review Phase

It is self-study or critical review that lays the basis for everything else that follows in the institutional master planning process. In the words of Hartman and Schell, "an institution must first determine what it is and where it has been *before* it can think about what it wants to be in the future." In order for this opening phase to net positive results, however, all of the principal players in this exercise—president, board of trustees, director, and staff—must approach it with a receptive and constructive attitude, as well as a sense of total commitment to the procedural format and the results, the remainder of the planning process that will follow, and the implementation of the final recommendations.

It is at this juncture, before the first phase even gets underway, that the director plays a vital role, working in concert with his board president to educate all participants in the process as to its purposes and its long-term merits. Through effective communications he can help to alleviate feelings of anxiety and intimidation that self-study often engenders, thereby assuring that the exercise will not be disruptive or destructive but will foster a positive atmosphere for institutional advancement. He must also underscore the importance of undertaking the task with complete candor; otherwise the institution will stand little chance of achieving the ultimate goal of the first or self-study phase—"institutional self-awareness" that will allow for planning "for both internal and external change" in the years ahead.[11] In my experience as a consultant to historical agencies, I have observed self-study endeavors in which sensitive or potentially embarrassing issues or topics have been glossed over or even completely ignored, much to the disadvantage of the entire planning effort.

Proper timing for effective self-study or critical review is absolutely essential. Hartman and Schell summarize well the appropriate circumstances for undertaking such an assessment:

> . . . an institution is ready for self-study when it has been doing its work long enough to merit evaluation, when there is a need for change, when there is a problem to be resolved, or when an institution needs to redirect its programs and resources.[12]

The planning process could be profitably commenced, therefore, at a number of convenient points in the varying life cycle of an institution—when new financial or collection resources come to the museum; when preparations are being made for AAM accreditation review; before physical expansion, renovation, or new "bricks and mortar" projects are undertaken; prior to launching a major capital campaign, whether or not it is directed toward the improvement of the physical plant; when financial resources are curtailed, calling for an adjustment in institutional priorities and possible cutbacks in programs and services; or, most important, when a change in directorship occurs, thereby giving the new incumbent an opportunity to participate in the creation of his own agenda.

I concur with Hartman and Schell that ideally the planning process, particularly the initial phase, should not take place when an institution is experiencing difficult times; but sometimes there is no other systematic way to resolve problems caused by leadership failures, the negative impact of external economic factors, man-made or natural disasters, etc., without doing this. It may be traumatic and stressful, but there may be no immediate alternative. At the least it is my firm view that master planning, and hence the self-study component, should take place every three to five years as Hartman and Schell urge. My years as a director have convinced me that it is very difficult to accurately project and prepare for an institution's future for any longer period, lacking foresight as to future unknown conditioning factors.

To ensure the best results the director should play a key role, working with his president and board of trustees, in establishing the functioning framework for the self-study phase and in determining who should participate and in what capacities. At the Essex Institute, where we undertook master planning in the early eighties, we established a board/ staff coordinating committee, under the president's chairmanship, for the self-study phase, much along the lines of the Hartman/Schell model. Rather than entrust full responsibility for this phase to a single central committee, however, we went one step beyond and appointed a series of working subcommittees or task forces, each chaired by a board member and each devoted to a single aspect of the institution's operation. With the full involvement of all board members, the entire staff, and pertinent outside resource people (institutional volunteers and members, community leaders, etc.), the subcommittees addressed such subject areas as governance, financial administration, institutional image and marketing, development, the museum program, the library, publications, the historic house properties, and facilities management and security.

Over a two to three month period these bodies met, provided verbal status reports at specially convened board meetings, and then drafted a set of final reports summarizing their findings and offering recommendations for consideration during the subsequent long-range planning phase. As institutional CEO I was asked to prepare a final self-study report that consolidated in one document the contents of the subcommittee reports. It was highly appropriate, I have always believed in retrospect, that I performed this nurturing, overseeing, and conceptualizing function; and I have since recommended this format for self-study, with subtle alterations, to other institutions. It gave me the opportunity to present my own views and personally help shape the future of an institution in which I had a direct stake.

The possible use of an outside consultant or consultants in the self-study or critical review phase is debatable. For some institutions this may be appropriate and workable, while for others it may be unnecessary or even counterproductive. What is self-study, after all, if it is not primarily generated by the institution itself and the people most directly associated with it? At the Essex Institute we chose to conduct our own exercise independently without the direct benefit of consultant expertise and guidance, and this approach worked extremely well. On the other hand, at another large historical institution with which I recently maintained a lengthy consulting relationship, board commitment to self-study or, for that matter, to the entire process of master planning was almost totally lacking; thus the director, much to his credit, after securing board endorsement, used consultant-directed self-study to lay the foundations for future long-range planning. It was really the only option he had at his disposal to encourage such vital activity. By taking this tack this director overcame the "why-don't-you-do-it-and-we'll-rubber-stamp-it" attitude of his board and took positive steps to move his institution forward.

There were deficiencies to this methodology (these were predictably built in from the onset), however, and the externally administered effort at self-study lacked sufficient credibility because of inadequate grassroots involvement on the part of the staff and the board itself. Plainly and simply, not enough people "bought into the process." Thus, while the board approved the results of critical review, it remained reluctant to enter actively into long-range planning, and despite what the director and staff could independently accomplish to realize progress, the institution for all intents and purposes remained dead in the water. In this instance, therefore, the use of consultants (I myself concentrated on the programmatic side, while others focused on financial administration and development) proved to be a mixed bag, though surely very little could have happened at all without our presence and involvement.

As Hartman and Schell so aptly point out in their essay, the scope of a self-study, whether it be all-encompassing or restricted to "fine tuning," is directly tied to the needs of the institution. The study's level of sophistication can easily be adjusted, depending on available time, people, and resources, to meet the requirements of large as well as small history museums. An effective self-study should start with programmatic evaluation and culminate with institutional analysis. Schell and Hartman recommend, therefore, that assessment concentrate on functions, rather than departments or divisions, and in this regard, admittedly, the Essex Institute exercise, in which the two were merged, may have been flawed.

Through the assessment, programs can be considered in relation to the "mission, priorities, resources, and operations of the whole institution," with a historical examination, the first step in fact-finding, providing the underpinnings of the process.[13] Those involved have the opportunity to back off, objectively scrutinize the institution, and pose and seek answers to fundamental questions that, in the flurry of daily operations, are usually ignored. All throughout self-study I urge the director's close attention and active participation. More often than not management issues are raised that not only bear on daily institutional operations, but more significantly, have long-term consequences for the future of the institution and that individual's ongoing role.

## Institutional Goal Setting Through the Long-Range Planning Phase

Upon the successful completion of self-study, the Hartman/Schell master planning model advances to the second major phase in which "changes and strategies are recommended for the future." Right at the beginning of this phase, the director's involvement is critical. In the ideal scenario, working with the president and board, he acts as the initiator and catalyst for this core portion of the planning process. As an initial step the enlightened director will encourage and help implement a brief period of preliminary planning (the "planning for planning" stage) during which an ad hoc steering committee (this could be the reconstituted and recharged coordinating committee of the dozen or so people employed in the self-study phase) of selected trustees and staff members is formed to develop a purpose and structure for long-range planning and "establish ground rules for its conduct."

As part of this preparation for the second phase, the institutional leadership should identify key discussion issues and problems requiring resolution. Preliminary planning should also focus on methodology, financial resources, participants, and timetable. Hartman and Schell suggest that all this be set to paper to provide a convenient road map for long-range planning, and this is a task that either a presidential appointee or the director himself could perform.

In their essay Hartman and Schell devote considerable space to the questions of who should be involved in creating the plan, and what should be their respective roles. Although they do not come right out and say so, strongly implied in their remarks is the assumption that these people should be essentially the same as those who executed the self-study or critical review phase—the president of the board, other trustees, the director and selected staff, and community representatives, the common denominator being that all, in one way or another will be affected by the outcome. Referring again to the case of the Essex Institute planning experience, we staffed the second phase much as we had the first, employing the same coordinating committee and subcommittees to build on the self-study product. In this instance continuity in roles proved to be a great asset, though in the second phase of the process we did place much greater reliance on the coordinating committee than in the first; and it was this body that assumed final responsibility for the goal-setting function, and, of course, for preparing the summary report.[14]

There are varying schools of thought as to what the proper role of the director should be in long-range planning undertaken for the institution that he heads. Some in the historical museum field contend that because the director is potentially vulnerable and must remain flexible, detached, receptive to change, and unfailingly committed to the process, he should not be the one to assume the leadership of the project. Sometimes the board president is charged with this responsibility; but unless this individual is an effective communicator, inspires broad respect, is unusually dedicated, and possesses a sound knowledge of the institution and others like it, such an arrangement is not apt to be successful. Another solution, as the Hartman/Schell model suggests, is for a senior administrator, such as an assistant director or department head, to serve in place of the director; and this certainly can work well depending on that individual's qualifications, and the status of his interpersonal relationships with trustees and other staff.

It is my personal preference, however, that the director himself assume the leadership role (with the endorsement of the board of trustees), for it is he more than anyone else who stands to be most directly affected by the final planning recommendations. It is only proper then that he be positioned at the heart of the process, as he will be chiefly responsible for implementing these recommendations and perpetuating the planning legacy in the life cycle of his institution while he serves as its director. But whoever is in charge, as Hartman and Schell observe, it is still incumbent on the director to keep the board informed on the progress of planning, alert the trustees to potentially sensitive issues, and prepare them for the recommendations and the consequences of implementation. It is also the director, more than anyone else, who is in the best position to assure an open-ended and democratic process through the full participation of staff, volunteers, members of the institution, and the public, particularly interested parties from the surrounding community.[15]

The issue of involvement of consultants or outside experts in long-range planning is, however, quite another matter, inspiring differing reactions. Those who advocate their use stress the value of having an outside perspective to help set the planning agenda, guide discussions and decision making, and add expertise on institutional functions that is not available from other participants. Unquestionably, their presence can serve to break down insularity and parochialism. On the other side of the argument, those who prefer not to use consultants in this phase of planning point to the expense, the problem of finding a suitable person or persons, and the desire not to "air the dirty linen" to those outside of the institutional "family." Should the history museum seek consulting assistance, however, the director will be responsible for maintaining close communications with those under contract, assuring that they meet the charge set for them by the coordinating committee. We did not choose to employ a consultant or consultants to assist in the long-range planning phase at the Essex Institute, and though we performed well procedurally, I think that our final recommendations could well have been strengthened by the presence of a noninstitutional point of view in the drafting deliberations.[16]

As Hartman and Schell further detail, the long-range planning phase, in order to be a valid exercise, must be founded on a solid research base. This calls for a comprehensive process of collecting and evaluating information from a variety of sources, including documents of institutional governance, operational policy statements, grant proposals, previous consultant reports, publications, financial documents, annual reports, statistical compilations, member and visitor survey data, meeting minutes, general museum literature, AAM MAP evaluation and accreditation review materials, reports on visits to other museums, and interviews with others associated with the institution but not intimately involved in the project. Of these sources grant proposals to the federally funded endowments and agencies (NEA, NEH, NSF, NHPRC, IMS), particularly the NEA and NEH "challenge" and the IMS general operating support programs, can be a tremendous aid in that they obligate applying institutions to amass great amounts of data and develop future plans, vital components of a long-range planning exercise.[17] A wise and competent director will prepare for institutional planning long in advance by identifying the research sources that undergird the long-range planning phase and by providing an initial impetus to tackle it imaginatively and productively.

Once a solid research base is in place, the planning team may proceed next to an examination of "the mission and purpose, goals, and objectives of the institution." No one who has ever been through it will deny that this is the most exciting and creative part of master planning. For it is at this pivotal stage that the sources generated by research are analyzed, new ideas and solutions devised, institutional priorities set, the costs of implementation estimated, and new funding possibilities studied. The director should be a central participant in the discussions, seizing on every possible opportunity to express his vision for his institution. While the substance of meetings should be documented and summarized in writing, it is perhaps best that the director himself not be saddled with this task, and that he remain free to contribute to the proceedings while another member of the coordinating committee takes on the secretarial job. Once recommendations have been finalized (and hopefully consensus has been achieved on these!), and the supporting rationale constructed for them, it is time to move on to the third and final phase of the process.[18]

## The Strategic Institutional Planning Phase

Many people in history museum work, when confronted with the term "strategic institutional planning" have only a bare idea of what it is. Others, though they may understand the meaning of the term, probably have never put this aspect of planning to use at their respective institutions. Because it is relatively new in nonprofit management circles and is still largely foreign to museums, only a small number of institutions in the history field are believed to have engaged in it to date. It has been the traditional habit of most planning teams, upon completion of the long-range planning phase of master planning, to stop right there, passing the final prioritized list of recommendations on to the leadership of the institution for implementation.

More often than not in such a scenario, this weighty responsibility falls exclusively to the director and staff, who may or may not receive the board support and involvement that they must have to do it well. This was certainly my experience at the Essex Institute where we did not consciously conduct strategic planning, and I suspect many other institutional heads have been faced with the same dilemma. Over the years I have come to the conclusion that it is very difficult, if not impossible, to carry out the recommendations resulting from long-range planning without benefit of the actions emanating from the strategic planning phase—the capstone to any successful master planning project. It has become literally the key to institutional survival in today's increasingly competitive nonprofit organizational world.

What then is this seemingly mysterious process that the management specialists customarily refer to as "strategic institutional planning"? In the words of Robert Simerly, from his article earlier cited, the strategic planning follow-up to long-range planning "emphasizes the process of implementing, through specific strategies, the plan as well as the product of the plan."[19] It is the systematic act of devising specific strategies to overcome resistance to change, as well as to initiate and deal with change, that Simerly feels distinguishes this type from all other facets of planning. It cannot succeed, though, without a great deal of cooperative hard work and interaction among board members, the director and other administrators, and the staff. As the major outgrowth of strategic planning, "staffing levels and responsibilities, budget needs, facility and equipment needs, and the timing for implementing each of the recommendations are specified."[20] It is, in short, the methodological means for accomplishing the goals and objectives conceived and promulgated by the previous phase of master planning.

To satisfy the human resources needs for the third phase, the Hartman/Schell model recommends utilizing the coordinating committee that orchestrated the long-range planning phase, but with the addition of those staff, if they are not already members, who will be primarily responsible for implementing the final recommendations. Again, as with the previous phase and for the same reasons, I advocate the designation of the director to chair the affairs of this committee, though in some instances, I grant that it may be more appropriate to have a senior staff person serve in this capacity. But whoever does this, he "must schedule regular meetings, make sure that deadlines are met, and keep the committee focused on the institution as a whole." I agree with Hartman and Schell that trustee participation is desirable, but that those involved must be constantly mindful of the distinction between policy-making and the staff implementation of policy that will follow the strategic planning phase.[21]

Hartman and Schell, as well as others, discuss the subject in some depth. At this juncture, therefore, I will offer only a passing view of what constitutes effective strategic planning; but I will reflect on where I think the director should properly fit in. In a nutshell strategic planning should review the second phase recommendations "accept or reject them, and devise a plan of action for each one it accepts." This inevitably will entail goal identification, the examination of alternative strategies, the development of appropriate actions to meet accepted goals, the specification of required human resources, the finalization of a time schedule, the identification of the "where and how" of each action, and, in the confirmation of work initiated in the previous phase, the definitive calculation of implementation expenses and the designation of funding sources, both internal or external. Thus, the committee will inevitably focus on programs, staff and volunteers, facilities, equipment, supplies and materials, costs, and income sources, in addition to the need for follow-up marketing and evaluation. With the advantage of his professional knowledge and experience, the director can assist immeasurably in this process by assuming a forceful, dynamic, and proactive posture, regardless of whether he serves as committee chair. The more senior and creditable he is in the field, the more valuable his contribution to the process is apt to be.

The director, in my view, should be a central figure in the preparation of the final master planning report, as well as in the dissemination of publicity about it. In fact in many cases it may be appropriate that he be *the* central figure in the performance of these tasks. If he has served as chair of the coordinating committee, it makes logical sense to have him draft the final report for submission to and final review by the coordinating committee, distribution to and official sanction from the full board of trustees, and circulation to the staff.

Once completed it becomes the document of the *entire* institution and all of its constituencies. The report, with supporting documentation, should summarize "what the institution is, what it wants to be, and how and when it will get there," given the availability of resources. It should include, as Hartman and Schell properly specify: an executive summary (cover sheet); an outline of content; a statement of purpose and methodology; an institutional history; a description of the institution's organization, collections, programs, and services; a commentary on institutional strengths and weaknesses; a needs assessment; a financial and fundraising analysis; an institutional mission statement; a list of institutional goals and objectives; a set of recommendations, in order of priority; a corresponding group of alternative implementation strategies; an implementation timetable in diagrammatic form; and appendices.

While such a comprehensive document is necessary for in-house use, an abbreviated version is more suitable for distribution to the media and the general public; oftentimes there can be great benefit to doing this, and an enterprising director can use the opportunity to gain positive publicity and attract new support for his institution. From my experience I believe it largely to the detriment of an institution to conceal the results of master planning, for in doing this the public trust is not fully satisfied.[22]

## Implementation

It is in the implementation of master planning that the director of a historical museum really earns his salary. In most instances of institutional master planning with which I am familiar, it is the director who has been entrusted with the responsibility for spearheading the execution of recommendations and "for monitoring the progress of the institution in carrying out the plan." This is a time-consuming and energy-sapping process—just ask any director who has been through it! Among the requisite talents and skills are diplomacy, persuasiveness, consistency, flexibility, resoluteness, integrity, and openness. Close relations, on an informal as well as on a regular reporting basis, should be maintained with the president and the full board of trustees; implementation will not go smoothly, or may even fail to achieve its goals if the director does not religiously attend to this. The same may be said for staff members, whose confidence in the planning outcome must be continually reinforced in order to assure their complete dedication to the implementation tasks that they will be called upon to perform.[23]

Planning should never stop at an institution, and master planning documents should be constantly reviewed and updated. Yet there are some people I have encountered in the museum field who seem to feel that once a three-to-five-year plan is in place, there is no need to look at it again critically until the next three-to-five-year planning cycle arrives. This brings to mind the image of the ostrich, head stuck in the sand while the world passes it by! It is the *obligation* of the director and board of trustees to make duly certain that the master plan remains a live document, always responsive to new internal and external influences as they may arise and impinge on the institution.

Enlightened leadership will insist on a regular, formalized update of the plan, perhaps on a yearly basis, with the setting of one-year action goals and implementation strategies, i.e., short-term operational planning. Annual monitoring reports should be compiled and submitted by the director. Boards of trustees should consider the establishment of a permanent planning committee (if the institution does not already have one in place) that can work with the director on the annual review, updating, and reporting processes, and, hence, enhance the experience and effectiveness of all who in one way or another serve the institution. And finally let us not overlook the members of the public, who, by virtue of such responsible and strong institutional commitment to planning, will be the fortunate beneficiaries of the highest quality programs and services that the history museum, continually reenergized, is able to deliver.

As you ponder the significance and implications of successful institutional planning, and the director's ideal role in it, recall briefly the opening image of the ship on a stormy sea, but on this occasion with its steering in good functioning order, making safe headway toward its final port of call. Equipped with the capacity to guide his vessel toward its ultimate goal, the captain is now able to exercise positive control over its long-term destiny. By virtue of regularly scheduled planning, so too will the leadership of a history museum be able to direct efficiently the institution toward realizable goals in fulfillment of its mission.

History museums all over the United States routinely and systematically should consider it mandatory to subject their current planning programs, whatever form they may assume, to the closest possible scrutiny and to consider ways in which their efforts at planning and self renewal can be improved. Institutions that have not previously engaged in organized planning should summon the energy and the means to do it at the next propitious moment. To the directors of such institutions particularly, I offer a few parting words about planning conveniently borrowed from the Madison Avenue realm of commercial advertising, "Try it! You'll like it!" But I warn you, be sure to do it prudently, for it could very possibly become habit-forming!

# 10

# The Director as Fund Raiser, Marketing Agent, and Cultivator of Institutional Support

by

Albert T. Klyberg

ALBERT T. KLYBERG has been the director of the Rhode Island Historical Society since 1969, prior to which time he was on the staff of the William L. Clements Library at the University of Michigan. He has taught at Brown University, Providence College, Rhode Island College, and the University of Rhode Island. He is a graduate of the College of Wooster, Wooster, Ohio, where he received an A.B. in history and economics, and of the University of Michigan which granted him an M.A. in history. Mr. Klyberg has served in the past as a member of the National Museum Services Board and of the Executive Committee and Council of AASLH.

Each time we open the door of our museum to a visitor, that person is not only the VIP who receives the story of our site, but he or she becomes a potential partner in the enterprise of sharing the story with those who came after. Cultivation for participation in the institution is part of every contact, and the director has to set the example. Rhode Island Historical Society director, Albert T. Klyberg, at the entrance to the John Brown House, Providence. Courtesy of John Miller Documents, Rhode Island Historical Society, Providence, Rhode Island.

## Tuxedos, Tin Cups, and Tambourines

*T*radition holds that one of the original uses for the academic hood was to house bread crusts and other rewards from begging for those moments of personal necessity when the scholar was otherwise not mentoring or professing. It is too bad historical agency directors do not have some similarly designed functional apparel.

Somehow a tin cup and a tambourine are awkward to manage in a tuxedo,[1] particularly if you are also encumbered by a tray of slides, flip charts, annual reports, audits, a letter from the IRS, and a model of your proposed building.

Not being acquainted by personal experience with a family environment beset by the relentless requirement to distribute excess wealth through charitable channels, I am still continually amazed by the "miracle" of fund raising, whereby one merely sends off a letter to a person or foundation requesting money for some project, and a check is duly returned in the mail. Amazing! Who would have thought it possible? Yet it happens every day.

As it turns out, it is not all that easy, but, in fact, it nearly is and the result is the same. There are, indeed, people and institutions that will give you money if you ask them in the right way. In fact they are in business to do just that. They are pleased to give money away, even relieved. It is important at the outset to state this very basic reality, because one of the biggest initial obstacles to overcome in fund raising is the natural embarrassment of the solicitor in approaching people to give money. If you know they are already disposed to dispose, then you are half way home.

If this miracle of modern-day loaves and fishes is true and so easy to work, then why are there so many worthy causes going unfulfilled? Why are museums and historical societies having tough times? Why are salary levels of their professionals so low? The answer is, of course, that the needs exceed the supply of support, and there are lots of factors involved in running a successful institutional development program. Professional donors do not usually give to people and programs they do not know and feel uncomfortable about. It can take a while to gain access to them, to educate them about needs, and to assure them that if they do give you the money, you will know how to use it effectively. However, all that does not change two of the basic realities—the first is that there really are people ready and eager to give just for the asking; and second, if you are the executive director of an institution, there is no way of avoiding being centrally involved in the asking process if you are going to be successful in institutional development.

The director of the institution is the person most donors expect to hear from or speak to. No matter what size development staff you have or the degree of its expertise, it is the director who is usually called upon to make the pitch that clinches the "sale." The director is viewed by most publics as the chief spokesperson, the intellectual leader, the "boss." Everyone wants to deal with the boss. It is a reality—accept it. This does not mean there is no role for a development officer or development staff—far from it. Having a good development office can be cost efficient in researching prospects and doing all the follow-up and recognition of donors so necessary if you are going to go back again. But in spite of the fact Brown University may have eighty-five people on its development staff, it is the president of the university who most often makes the key pitch. In the cases where that does not happen the key requester is a close friend of the prospect or the volunteer chair of the campaign.

Throughout the course of this discussion, from here on in, I intend to use the broader term, *development*, rather than *fund raising*. The intent here is not to slip into something more euphemistically comfortable. If anything, I want to avoid euphemism and advocate candor, directness, and simplicity. I want to argue that it is desirable to avoid ultrasuede if cotton is available. I want to use *development* because it is a more comprehensive term. Fund raising is short-term. It is a tactic. Development is a strategy. Fund raising deals with a single event. Development involves a whole series of factors. Because fund raising is so often such a specific action if it is carried out in isolation to an institution's mission, it can sometimes backfire. Be careful what you ask for—you might just get it. Development should be accepted and treated by the staff and trustees of an institution as a long-term, ongoing process, not a series of stunts to raise money to pay next month's or next year's bills.

To be successful a development program has to have most of the following elements in place *before* requests for support are made:

- A clearly defined mission statement and a well-articulated set of institutional goals and programs.
- A multiyear (long-range) plan.
- Reports, reviews, and appraisals rendered by independent outsiders attesting to management's ability to run the place, and a validation of the institution's integrity. These can be financial audits, accreditation certificates, MAP reports, public press notices, or peer reviews of programs (preferably all of the above).
- The ability to state and document a compelling case of need, including what the proposed project seeks to accomplish, who is going to carry it out, over what period of time and at what cost, and who will be the beneficiaries.

- A community representative support group or board.
- Competent professional staff.

The reason why most, if not all, of the above have to be in place is because these are the common standards used by funding sources for philanthropic giving. Donors seek assurances of standards of organization, expertise, and responsibility. They want to minimize the risk of giving to places that are going to fail. That is why Harvard University has more than a billion dollars in its endowment and a little college a few miles away goes out of existence. Well, that is not the entire reason, actually. Other important factors are length of time in the field, consistency in delivering services, and cultivation of prospects over time.

Cultivation begins with institutional integrity. Integrity is not just a condition necessary for development. It is a central character trait of the institution. It is why distinguished people are willing to serve on your board, why people are willing to entrust family heirlooms to your care, and why government agencies are willing to grant charters and exemptions. There must be confidence in the institution. This confidence derives from a respect for its leadership, the way in which the institution conducts its financial affairs, and the quality of its programs and services. All of the clever marketing in the world cannot substitute for this basic asset. Either you have it, or you do not.

Integrity stems from living up to promises made to previous donors to conserve collections. It means having written policies and procedures that are observed consistently in daily activity. It means being free from conflicts of interest; it means a seriousness of purpose, of accountability. It means all of the old Roman virtues of civic trust: gravity (seriousness), authority (wise leadership), science (knowledge), and *veritas* (truthfulness). Public reputation and perceptions are critical first steps for any development program.

Long-term cultivation, the building of friendships, and letting people get to know you constitute another key factor. Fifteen years ago the Rhode Island Historical Society was given the home of United States Senator Nelson Aldrich by his son, Winthrop W. Aldrich, former American ambassador to Great Britain and president of the Chase Manhattan Bank. Mr. Aldrich arranged with his nephews, the Rockefeller brothers, to endow the house. I never met Mr. Aldrich; he died before all the details were completed, and we worked those out with his attorney and his daughter. So far as I know my only contact with him was a note he wrote thanking me for sending him a print of early nineteenth-century Providence. The print was a promotional piece, a beautiful watercolor that we sent to our members, out-of-the-blue, to alert them to an exhibition of our paintings to be held at Brown University as part of the society's

150th anniversary. Ironically, the reason we held the exhibit at Brown was because we had no gallery space of our own for changing shows. Mr. Aldrich's gift gave us that place. But the cultivation began with a casual contact. Some fund raising consultants have likened the process to scattering seeds.

The vital adjunct to this seed scattering, though, is the ability to add nourishment and to be able to respond quickly if something sprouts. That is why having a clear idea of mission and having a plan is so important. When Mr. Aldrich's attorney asked us one weekend what we would do with his house and property if it were offered to us, we were able by the middle of the next week to supply him with a seven- or eight-page outline of our need for exhibition space and a lecture hall, the kinds of programs we could offer the community that would be unique in Providence, and how much endowment would be necessary to carry all this out. Furthermore, we were able to make a strong case for our worthiness based on a track record of a century and a half and could cite a dozen mutual connections of the historical society with Mr. Aldrich's known interests.

The general outlines of that case had been developed years before without Mr. Aldrich's gift in mind. They were part of our long-range plan. The general cultivation of our membership had also proceeded several years before. When the opportunity presented itself, however, we pulled the framework of our case together in a matter of hours. It was not all settled immediately. All kinds of revisions had to be made to our plans for the house. We debated the budget and size of endowment. We underwent scrutiny by the Rockefeller Brothers Fund staff. Various bonafides had to be presented. A certain amount of luck and timing was involved, too; we were in competition with Brown University and the Rhode Island School of Design. But to the degree we had planned ahead, we had made our own luck.

Outside consultants for a development program are a desirable element in the cultivation process. Before beginning a major capital campaign or annual giving program, it is customary to hire a fund-raising firm to do a feasibility study. Prospective donors will often react candidly to these firms. The purpose of the study is to determine how ready the organization is for its campaign, how well it is respected in the community, and whether or not the "usual prospects" will respond. Such a study can help determine how large the campaign and who its leadership should be if it is going to have a chance of succeeding. Another service of a fund-raising consultant, particularly a local one, can be an honest review of what other campaigns are taking place at the same time and where your institution will fit in with heavier traffic. Prospective donors, identified by the institution as the most likely prospects, are asked by the consultant for their opinions of the institution, their degree of enthusiasm for the proposed campaign,and an indication of the size of their gifts and a willingness to solicit their friends.

Again, because the director is the logical person whose various roles put him or her at the intersections of board policy and staff programs, he/she is usually the most visible person to the community. Many of the reactions of potential donors, fairly or unfairly, become a report card on how well the director is perceived to manage the institution. Directors need to be able to deal with that scrutiny. Success in that regard usually begins with the initial recognition that the responsibility for development is a central, not a peripheral one. One needs to schedule it into the work day; do not cram it in as an unwanted interruption or distraction. More to the point, the director's role in cultivation and development should be a positive proactive one. If this is the case, it is less likely the institution will be blind sided or co-opted by an aggressive donor's agenda. It should always be the institution's agenda, not the donor's, that is on the development table. The director can do much to see that the programs and purposes of the institution do not get distorted or perverted in the promotional and development processes.

Consistency and repetition are vital in cultivation. As one of my trustees who was in the advertising business once admonished, "Remember, you are talking to a passing parade." You cannot stop asking for people to join, and you can never thank people enough for helping out. We continually encounter people who have never heard our message before or who were not paying attention the first or second time we talked to them. One of the successful major museums hereabouts has used as many as seven letters in a series for its membership recruiting device. These letters were not just appeals to join, but interesting and intriguing messages using history cleverly and persuasively to interest the prospect. Most people join by the time they receive numbers four or five.

The sequential and expansive dimensions of cultivation are other principles to keep in mind. We all strive to attract visitors to our institutions. Admission fees and sales-desk proceeds offset some of the cost of getting the visitor into the door. Cultivating the visitor's interest to return to the institution should be a part of the first visit. Furthermore, an extension of the institution's hospitality ought to be a gracious invitation to join the organization as a member. The suggestion ought to stress that members participate in the excitement and satisfaction of being part of the enterprise of saving and sharing a people's history.

If an institution is doing a good job in presenting its public programs, the museum or historical society should never be more attractive and alluring than when the visitor is on its premises. After someone has had a energizing and enlightening exhibition experience is a great time to invite them to join. There is something drastically wrong with your museum if your best membership recruiting program is one based on sending mass mailings to total strangers on purchased lists. The satisfied visitor, at hand, on your premises ought to be your best prospect.

Then the cultivation sequence and expansion of involvement should begin as one is drawn from being a new member to a volunteer, to an annual donor, to a service committee member, to a trustee, or member of a special collector's circle, to, finally, a member of a wills and bequest program. I estimate that for every ten thousand visitors paying general admission, one thousand could be interested in joining as members. I estimate a third of these general members can be converted into annual givers, and one hundred of the one thousand members can be recruited as volunteers. Thirty of these new one thousand members are prospects for a gift or bequest. It is only logical, then, that if this sequence is going to work as an institutional financial food chain, the director needs to see that the first links in that chain—the volunteer docents, the gallery guards, and the telephone receptionists—are as well motivated and informed about the institution and its desire and need to attract members as is possible.

Brilliant strategies in the executive offices are only as good as the actions on the front-line of public contact. More gifts have come to museums because of friendly guards or enthusiastic tour guides than most development officers would like to admit. How well are these people motivated in you institution? Does the end of your typical tour end with a whimper or a bang?

A good part of a successful development program is understanding the psychology of what makes people want to give. This is as important as knowing the likely prospects. People give because they become convinced of a need. People give upon the advice of others, their friends, and community leaders of stature whom they respect. People give out of loyalty to a cause, a fondness for a community or place, and out of a sense of duty to family forebears or ethnic group. All of these motives can be worked into a successful development program.

One of the reasons development takes longer than fund raising is the amount of time it takes to do research on people's interests and match them to the institution's needs. It takes time to build real friendships, to allow people to buy into programs. There is a direct relationship of developmental success to donor involvement. There are obvious areas of institutional work where amateurs should not replace professionals, but the institution that makes no room for amateur involvement is going to have a tough time raising support. Again, with proper planning and imagination, meaningful, satisfying work can be found for the volunteer. An institution that only wants members for their money misses out on the magic of collaboration and comes across as exclusionary. Properly alerted, members can be a field army tipping off curators to important collections, and creating interest and good will. Organizations that believe they can ignore the long haul of development and cultivation by simply hiring high-priced fund-raising counsel for a particular campaign, or by setting up a development office with staff fund raisers alone, are kidding themselves. There has to be direct institutional involvement by the board and top staff in development. There has to be an involved membership as well.

Another form of self-delusion is that doing fund raising is cheap. Development offices are expensive. Cultivation is expensive. Keeping an office and program going and sustained over time is expensive. There are no easy shortcuts; there are also no automatic rewards. Every tree does not grow in heaven. All we can say is that history shows that long-term comprehensive plans and strategies show better results than short-term fits and starts.

This might be a good place to comment about the attractiveness of history as a discipline and historical agencies as magnets for money. A little perspective is in order. History institutions are not in the same development ranks as religious bodies, hospitals, schools, and colleges. Very few of life's central dramas get carried out on our stage, at least not on purpose. Most of the philanthropic dollars will flow to places where people are born, educated, healed, or theologically inspired, no matter what we do. It means we often have to wait our turn somewhat down the agenda from other community needs.

I can recall waiting an entire year for just three minutes of opportunity to plead the historical society's case to the governor or to have a few moments to appear before the Finance Committee in the state's House of Representatives. Nonetheless, we have to be ready to put forth our very best arguments in just those three or four minutes. We have to be interesting, surprising, earnest, and precise. Over the years I have discovered that history does have compelling arguments, and some of the most successful ones are offered for your adaptation.

A frequent question asked of me is just what is it, exactly, that the historical society does. The temptation is to talk about publishing history, running a research library, putting on exhibits and offering school programs, but to governors or legislators wrestling with medical waste fouling the beaches, teacher strikes, or inmate uprisings at the state prison, somehow talking about the details of the historical society sounds nice but not necessary. It takes on a slightly different magnitude, however, if you remind them of the personal agony and tragedy when a family member is struck down by memory loss. Then, you suggest that communities and states are in danger of losing their memories, too, with an equal amount of pain and disruption. What it is, then, that the historical society really does is to insure that the community does not lose its memory. In a sense the society becomes the community memory. Of course, if that really is not the case in your community and everybody knows it, or if you are the memory for only one part of the community, you do not have as strong a case.

Another argument people understand is that although we are given a lot of collections for free, the real cost is keeping something safe forever. There are enough well known stories of art loss and irreversible collection deterioration to illustrate the point. The fact that as many people visit museums as attend sports events seems to catch people's attention, though frankly I have never known the origin of that statistic.

Years ago when I first went up to the state legislature to see if we could get an increase in our $21 thousand appropriation, I had totally misread the situation. Early in the session a friend and I spoke to his local legislator who introduced us briefly to the chairman of the House Finance Committee who was a used car salesman. He listened to our feeble explanation about how worthy our historical research library was, said he would see about helping us, and then went on his way, making the rounds of the lobby.

We had not researched our case very well. The people we trusted to carry it for us were indifferent to its merit and the budget went through without our increase. In our innocence we requested a meeting with the speaker who took time from his busy law practice to explain the way the House worked and the impossibility of reconsidering anything once the budget went to the Senate. He asked us about our programs, however. He asked what elements would appeal to the average member of the House. What was in our offerings that would appeal to their constituents? Did our programs truly appeal to the entire state population and the entire history of the state or only to the colonial period and the descendants of the first families?

We took his advice to heart. In subsequent years we made sure the breadth of our program was both genuine and well appreciated. We began a labor union archives, collected twentieth-century materials—TV films, and women's organization records. We sponsored the formation of a Black Heritage Society. These innovations were sincerely needed, and we had an exciting time doing them. The community acknowledged and rewarded the efforts, too. We did not depend on just one or two legislators. Eventually nearly 30 of the 150 senators and representatives would become members or friends of the society. We opened our facilities to state agencies and commissions. We took on assignments from the governor. Our appropriation climbed accordingly, growing over two decades from $21,000 to more than $300,000. Of course it did not hurt that my inexperienced friend who went with me to see the speaker eventually became speaker of the House himself.

Over the years, there have been some other telling points that seem to have hit the mark when trying to catch the attention of governmental officials. One of these is the notion that there are three essential elements to effective government: leadership, money, and information. Information is one of the things historical agencies are all about. The cumulative record of government—past leadership and prior decisions—can be an important resource in the decisions of current governmental activities. Those of us who manage archives or hold significant research collections have a resource of value to governors, legislatures, and administrative departments. We have made sure that the use of these resources by agencies and policy makers has been noted by our funding sources. Once we put ourselves on a footing other than just being one more "charity" with our hand out, financial aid can be justified as a cost of government.

Private/public partnerships has been another selling point. We have demonstrated that assigning tasks to us can be an efficient way for government to get things done—historical research, book publishing, and staffing public celebrations. Another point that has received recognition is the role of museums in providing life-long learning. Lastly, dramatizing the rescue of community treasures and heritage from oblivion gets a lot of mileage. The point, is you cannot be shy about telling people when you make a cultural rescue, as in the case when I walked into the governor's office and presented him with two volumes of colonial supreme court records that had been in the state's care but somehow had made it into the hands of an out-of-state antique dealer. We bought them and returned them with a flourish. My favorite headline in this regard was one we achieved by assuming temporary custody of a deaccessioned light house in order to prevent it from being vandalized. The headline read, "Historical Society Rescues Coast Guard."

Dramatic and clever use of opportunities is one way to stay in the public eye, an important adjunct to any development program. But press agentry and publicity stunts are a risky gambit and rarely can be sustained over time. What can be sustained over time are good notices and reviews of exhibits and publications. A little used and not very expensive visibility grabber is the creation of feature articles for distribution to local newspapers, replete with ready-to-use already captioned photos. During our state's 350th celebration, we furnished fifteen local newspapers with twelve monthly installments of a state history, along with locality-specific sidebars all for a total expense of some $4,000, which we garnered from an IMS grant. Some of the newspapers ran the stories as full-page features with the society's logo prominently displayed in color.

Keeping the organization in the public eye by sending out wave after wave of press release ripples designed to cultivate public esteem is the necessary background to a successful and sustained development program. This kind of cultivation can be done by development staff or volunteers with media experience. Just as board members and campaign volunteers can prepare a prospect with an endorsing good word in the end, however, it's either the director, the president of the board, or the chairman of the campaign who will make the big request in nearly all situations. As suggested a thorough understanding of the institutional purpose and needs is part of that preparation. Equally important is the research into the prospect's interests to match his or her need to give or interest in giving. Personal life circumstances in the prospect's background can make the timing either good or bad—a recent inheritance, the sale of a business, a divorce, or a death.

Ultimately, though, it comes down to a few words and the genuine, earnest enthusiasm with which they are delivered. Setting, circumstances, or who else accompanies the director when he or she makes the call are all dictated by the strategy as to what would comprise the perfect way to ask the question. One already knows from a variety of intelligence sources what are the areas of common interest as well as what topics to avoid. And then there is the pitch—one of perhaps three or four that can be appropriate. They are all related to what the organization is about:

1. The transmission from one generation to another of a community's treasures, community-prized mementos, and evidence of everyday life.
2. The need to care for and preserve these things indefinitely.
3. The capability to interpret and present them in intriguing and informative ways—every age of the community's past, for people of every age.
4. The significant and special qualities of history as a humanizing discipline, as a form of cultural literacy, and, conversely, the problems of illiteracy that result when it is neglected.

The question of how the prospective donor can aid the cause of history has to be phrased simply and the reasons for doing it made as powerfully as possible. It can require hours of preparation for a few minutes of conversation. The requirements are virtually the same for grant writing to foundations or budget presentations to public bodies: precise, jargon-free language; the use of interesting, fresh, and appropriate examples or metaphors; sincere, earnest case making, as free as possible from exaggeration or distortion—in other words the same kind of balance and integrity used in the best scholarly exposition. History has some powerful cards to play. Some donors are very interested in doing something to promote the survival of tradition (remember, tradition is the democracy we grant to the dead). Others want to aid education in nontraditional formats or settings. Personal association with historic sites or programs is attractive to many egos. Furthermore, one of the advantages of having memberships with high average ages is the opportunity to talk about bequests to people who are ready to make that decision. Many of these people are ready to consider "their" place in history. People also like to be associated with "real" treasures and their "home" town. A personal association with the real "stuff" of history—documents and artifacts, the symbols and emblems of America—holds enormous attraction.

What happens after you leave the visit is almost as important as the visit. Follow through and follow-up, good records, and appropriate recognition mean you can come back. Also an evaluation of the visit and its results is part of the permanent cultivation file. Development research is hard to come by; do not throw away information or experience that can be used again. Be prepared to tell your prospective donor what your track record is in carrying out other donors' wishes. Tell, discreetly, what others have done as a way of showing examples. No one wants to think they are the only "soft touch" in town. Work out a logical sequence of approaching people so that the logical top-pyramid people give first.

How is all this going to change, if at all, in the future? Although most of us were trained to analyze the past, and although Churchill once observed that the deeper one looks into the past, the further one can see into the future, we spend a great deal of our time as administrators living in the future of our expectations and anticipations. Ten years ago I thought I would spend some productive hours while snowbound in my office for about a week during the Blizzard of 1978. I got out all the program descriptions for NEH and NEA, the IMS guidelines and the *Foundation Directory,* along with various regional and state counterparts. On 5 x 8-inch file cards I cross-indexed all these sources and color-coded them to our society's projects and capital needs. This "dynamite" tool was good for about a year and a half. The Reagan Revolution hit Washington, shook up most of the agencies we had gotten to know, and made my index little more than a cultural artifact. So much for preparing for the future.

My guess is that within a year we will see new or expanded grant opportunities in Washington, just about the time when the full implications for charitable giving of the new tax reform act slow down private and corporate giving. In reviewing the admonitions and suggestions of my colleagues in the surrounding chapters of this work, I suspect if much of their advice and mine is taken to heart, directors will be more over-burdened with responsibilities and detail than before. I do not know how anyone can handle all this advice, at least not at the same time. I suggest then that directors in the future will have to work out very specific job descriptions and expectations with their boards. Institutions will need multi-year plans with a different administrative emphasis in different years in order to deal with all of the many assignments. And that, in larger institutions, the use of deputy directors will increase as will the necessity for the directors to delegate almost all detail work to responsible subordinates. Development and public relations offices will have to be permanent parts of the institution. The director's job will be very much like that of being president of a small college.

One of my favorite examples of the model director performing the cultivation function is my counterpart at the local museum of art. Nearly every day he takes the bus the fifteen blocks between his house and the museum. On more than one occasion he has walked the aisle of the bus handing out flyers about the current or up-coming show. More important than his chutzpah in accosting dazed commuters is the endearing, overwhelming charm of this man who is so obviously in love with his subject that he bursts with enthusiasm and captivates willingly an audience that is already semicaptive. Being with him must be a little bit like being with Teddy Roosevelt. His shouts of *marvelous, fantastic!* are so obviously sincere and unaffected that you want to jump off the bus and follow him right into the museum. He is a tribute to his grandfather, Harvard's museum master, Paul Sachs.

Quite frequently, when I am asked what I do for a career and answer that I direct a historical society, the next question usually is whether that is a part-time or volunteer job. The inquirer is nearly always dumfounded when I answer that it is more than full-time, and that I have the help of thirty full-time professionals to boot. This exchange is a pretty fair gauge as to the average public understanding of historical agencies. It is also at this very point almost daily that we begin institutional development and cultivation.

# 11

# The Diamond Link The Director as Internal Communicator

by

Susan Stitt

SUSAN STITT is president and chief executive of the Historical Society of Pennsylvania in Philadelphia. She served as director of the Museums at Stony Brook, New York, for fourteen years beginning in 1974. Her previous museum experience occurred at Old Sturbridge Village, Massachusetts; The Brooklyn Museum, New York; the Museum of Early Southern Decorative Arts, Old Salem, Inc., North Carolina; the Museum of the Albermarle, North Carolina; and the Historical Society of Pennsylvania. She holds a B.A. in American history from the College of William and Mary and an M.A. in American civilization from the University of Pennsylvania. Her many contributions to the museum field include leadership responsibilities with the American Association of Museums, the Mid–Atlantic Association of Museums, and the New York State Association of Museums.

Susan Stitt, former Director of The Museums at Stony Brook, addresses a group of trustees, staff, and members in February 1984. Seated to her left are Mrs. Peter J. Costigan,
chair of the board of trustees, and Mrs. Ward W. Melville, chair emerita, whose nine-
tieth birthday prompted the event illustrated. Courtesy of The Museums at Stony Brook,
Stony Brook, New York.

## The Diamond Link

*2*magine a triangle on a flat surface. Now imagine a second triangle above it, but upside down. Balance the point of the second on the point of the first. Then let the second triangle slide down into the first, just a little. The small diamond-shaped intersection that is formed is a museum director, the link between the trustees above, pyramidally structured, and the staff below, similarly organized.

If successfully balanced, the linkage between a museum's trustees and staff should be analagous to a diamond, a strong and valuable connection. Unsuccessfully balanced and controlled, these two units—the institution's human resources that animate and implement the museum's mission—can penetrate each other's functions sharply or begin to parallel each other, forming a slanted figure that lacks the aerodynamics to move the institution. A museum director's primary function is to enable a museum's trustees and staff to be effective in implementing the museum's mission by envisioning that institutional potential and communicating it in such a way as to make that vision theirs.

Initially, trustees and staff may seem so different as groups of people associated with a museum that different techniques would appear to be necessary to work effectively with the two. Unpaid, the trustees are volunteers who have agreed upon their election to become the corporation that is the museum. They are legally accountable as the museum's fiduciaries. The required perspective is broad. Demographically, trustees are usually community based and tend to be older and more established than the staff; these are the characteristics necessary to furnish the leadership and personal power essential for an effective trustee.

In contrast, the staff are likely to be young due to the limitations of the wage scale within the field to retain and attract equally qualified, more experienced workers; consequently, the museum's employees are less established and socially powerful. Generally half or more of the staff will be community based, half or less will be specialists brought to the institution because of certain skills and training, and half of the latter group will be entry level workers.[1] Functionally responsible and focused staff members, other than senior management, generally do not have the broad institutional perspective essential for trustees, and although desirable, it is not necessary for their adequate performance that they develop such an overview.

Key similarities unite trustees and staff. Foremost is attention to the institution. Whether unpaid or paid, both groups of people are obliged by the terms of their association to be attentive to the museum's needs and to its public responsibilities. Additionally, both have a duty of loyalty to the institution. But as attentive and loyal as both may be obliged to be neither can adequately understand the desirable result from their attention without information and leadership from the director—the diamond link. That information is not factual but is the interpretation of facts and circumstances as related to the museum's mission—its *raison d'etre*. It is this vision of the institution that requires attention and commands loyalty.

Ideally, the director's communication with new trustees begins before their election, when as members of the museum's community, they became interested, then involved, then committed to the institution. The way the museum presented itself in programs and in print formed an image that attracted their attention and sparked their interest. More often than should be the case, however, prospective trustees are not yet involved in the institution. As persons of influence and power, they are viewed as potentially useful trustees, persons who could, if they wished, be important to the museum. In this instance, as in the former, more desirable scenario, the museum's nominating committee initiates the relationship. If the director has infused these trustees with enthusiasm for the museum and respect for the obligations of trusteeship, this initial presentation should be illustrative of the nature of trusteeship.

Generally, the nontrustee director is expressly barred in the museum's bylaws from being an *ex-officio* member of the nominating committee because the duty to perpetuate continuous stewardship is not one that trustees can delegate. In this area, however, as in all others, it is important that the director, attending these meetings by invitation, be candid and forthright about the museum's needs in order to assist the trustees in developing an appropriate profile for prospective trustees and a job description for their role within the organization. Although it is obvious that no one can make a responsible decision about the commitment of becoming a museum trustee without an honest presentation of the standards of care and amount of time involved, it is too often true that the anxious nominating committee chair, to avoid rejection, minimizes the time and attention needed from trustees, presenting thereby an inaccurate understanding of the necessary commitment. Whether or not this has been the case, the director's first official communication with new trustees is very important.[2]

An orientation packet of materials for and about the museum or board book of policies and procedures should be the talking piece for this director/trustee conference, but the real message is the museum's oral tradition, its self identification, and its mission, goals, and objectives. Orientation is vital to a trustee's effectiveness. No knowledge should be assumed. A clear picture of organizational dynamics must be traced. This meeting tests the director's skill as an interpreter, for time is always limited, and the range of information to be covered and facilities to be toured is large, whatever the size of the institution.

It is helpful for every museum director to be a trustee of some organization and through that experience to learn how difficult it is for a part-time volunteer to develop an accurate picture of an institution with its mission and goals in sharp focus. Being a trustee as part of leadership training is the best way for a museum director to learn the importance of separating essential issues and policy considerations from the operational concerns that can obscure any issue with their comforting and comfortable simplicity.

As the museum professional, the director is responsible for making sure that trustees and staff understand professional standards and know the reasons why the field has identified certain ethical principles concerning the governance and management of museums. Providing information on concerns within the museum field and within the museum is an important responsibility of the museum director, one of the key responsibilities. Once a museum's trustee asked me, "How would I have known what question to ask?" Gently but continuously, a responsible museum director instructs trustees about the questions to ask of their museum while providing the facts and the interpretation of those facts necessary to answer those questions and others.

The methods a director may use to interpret and inform are as diverse as the varied styles of management effectively employed in the field today. Background papers on issues, well documented board meeting packets, program presentations on exhibitions, or research reports during board meetings—all of these are useful communication techniques. Because people learn in different ways, care must be taken to provide information in varied formats. Some people are careful listeners, some are not; others read with understanding, others do not. As an educator, the director must never forget the importance of repetition.

The trustees, staff, and other people within a museum organization are at different stages of personal and professional growth and of understanding their museum. To the recently elected or appointed, the moral demonstrated by a situation five years ago is new. Nuances of the museum's financial condition are lost to an individual still struggling to understand the basic information on the balance sheet. Although a director may hire staff that share similar values, that professional compatibility is not as certain between the director and trustees. The director must be ever articulate about the museum's mission and goals, institutional heritage, and public responsibility to insure that trustees share perspective and priorities for the museum.

Communication and management of staff are at once more simple and more complicated than they are for the handling of trustees. Yet the same principles apply. Values must be shared, as must understanding of the museum's basic rationale. Once more, selection of appropriate individuals who have been given sufficient information to make an informed judgment is followed by orientation reinforced with continuous interpretation of standards, facts, and circumstances. Similarly, effective instruction is provided in varied formats—job descriptions, personnel manuals, memos, meetings, and newsletters. Perhaps more than is true with trustees, the director also communicates by example. Everyone, no matter how illiterate or unsophisticated about museums or inexperienced with vocational skills, reads body language with a high degree of accuracy and can observe the way in which a person works even if the motives and management techniques of that work are not understood. For staff in particular, a significant part of the message is the manner in which it is given.

Once a museum reaches the size in which it is necessary to involve someone other than the director as a supervisor, communication within the organization becomes more complicated and, without care, less effective. The problems increase arithmetically with the number of supervisors, each of whom expresses the same information differently. Verbal and nonverbal communication becomes less unified; there is more opportunity for confusion. It is no wonder that the staff of the nation's smaller museums include some of the most satisfied museum workers, for they work in an environment in which shared values and goals are most likely to exist and in which each worker has direct contact with their museum's product.

When there are multiple supervisors, formal management tools provide the best unifying techniques. A position description for each employee clarifies the relationship between that individual's work and the museum's purposes and responsibilities. The personnel manual contains, in addition to personnel policies and procedures, a history and description of the museum. The ethics policy states principles and procedures to assure adherence to behavioral standards. The collection management policy defines the characteristics of the artifacts that are the core of the museum's *raison d'etre* in addition to outlining the procedures approved for managing the collection. Care must be taken to insure that these tools are kept up to date and that each harried supervisor remembers to use them. Annual performance evaluations provide the opportunity, on a one-to-one basis, to restate the overriding concerns of the museum and relate them to each employee's objectives.

Ways to lessen the distance between staff and the director must be employed, even knowing that none of them are perfect. Informal meetings, notes in the staff newsletter, and social occasions now and then all help, as does acknowledging and occasionally employing informal networks. Setting aside a commons area in which staff from different segments of the museum may meet and share information strengthens these informal networks and creates new ones that traverse functional grouping. Most important, however, is making sure that the supervisors, who are supervised by the director, are taught continuously to understand the museum's mission and goals and the relationship of all activities to those paramount tenets. Once again, ways to do this are as varied as individuals who serve as directors. Care must be taken to avoid the application of this staff quote to any director's communication skills or lack thereof: "He played his cards so close to his chest that we weren't sure that even he knew what they were!"

It is one thing to recommend consistent and ongoing interpretation of a museum's mission and goals as the director's key principle for effective personnel management of both trustees and staff; it is another to be that primary interpreter of the museum to the museum as well as to society at large. Why are museum directors often less than perfect personnel managers—flawed diamonds?

No one can communicate an institution's mission if that mission is not understood. It is not necessary that the director always be the one who develops the brief sentence or two that express the museum's *raison d'etre*. It is necessary, however, that the director be able, in the diverse tongues and accents of the museum's trustees and staff, to express that mission. For such expression to be apt it must relate to the subject at hand, the current problem, the forthcoming opportunity. A person who doesn't understand can't explain and has difficulty relating paramount values to discrete situations. Each director must be able to develop and to defend the reason why the museum, for which that director is responsible, exists. Such a definition must be based on facts and institutional history upon which reasonable people may agree.

Some directors don't see their role as interpreting the mission of the museum. These individuals are content to manage rather than to direct and lead. The responsibility for institutional definition may be delegated to staff or abdicated to the board. Since communication between these two groups is through the director, such delegation or abdication may have the effect of only one-half or neither part of the organization understanding the mission—the reason for the organization. Decisions based upon differing criteria usually conflict. Institutions in which the director does not exercise the responsibility to express mission become troubled. Such conflict often becomes personal, as there is no shared ideological base. Most frequently, however, the director understands the mission and is theoretically willing to express it, but often is too uncomfortable in working situations to do so. Such insecurity may result in misinterpretations of the mission not being corrected or improvements not being accepted. The bombast of many museum directors veils their lack of operational courage.

Most adults harbor insecurities of one sort or another. Unfortunately there are significant reasons why certain insecurities may ever be in a museum director's consciousness. The terms of employment for most museum directors are not clearly stated in a contract or even, in too many cases, in a job description. Usually the position description is implicit; the assumption is that the director is in charge of day-to-day management and long-term strategic planning. Add a problem to this nonconsidered situation, whether that problem is a controversial exhibition or deaccession or inadequate cash flow in a perennially underfunded situation; add any problem and the normally comfortable reliance on the director may become uncomfortable. The question of who was to inform, who to ask, and who to decide becomes unanswerable in these strained circumstances. Museum trustees are usually most reluctant to evaluate their own performance and that of their peers and are remiss in monitoring the director's performance, compensation, and benefits regularly and professionally.

In this situation the director is expected to be self monitoring, to develop and enforce personnel policies for the staff, and self-administer those policies in a disinterested manner. An individual in this situation may develop patterns of self-interest and thereby become vulnerable to criticism or, and more frequently, tend to disadvantage himself or herself in a genuine effort to be beyond reproach and avoid not only a conflict of interest but the appearance of a conflict. Even if a director does not become disadvantaged in the honest effort to avoid self-dealing, the paramount duty of loyalty to the institution may have the effect of disadvantaging the director as, for example, earned vacation time is deferred in deference to the museum's schedule and needs, and extra time is contributed to compensate for insufficient staffing. Under the circumstances, the blurry nature of equitable compensation and benefits gives the director economic insecurity in a field in which compensation and benefits are known to be below average for comparable positions of responsibility requiring similar experience and educational credentials within a community. This economic insecurity is compounded by the fact that there is usually only one position for a museum director in a locality and, therefore, the expense and personal stress of relocation is necessary to continue employment within the field.

In addition to these financial problems and liabilities, as employees most museum directors have very fragile job security. Without a contract or regularly reviewed set of goals and objectives, directors are subject to, and too often subjected to, dismissal either without cause or with a cause that exists only because the trustees did not fulfill their responsibility to monitor and to evaluate the director, the museum's primary employee. The geometric picture of the museum's organization described at the beginning of this essay illustrates the lonely position of the museum's director, linking the pyramidally structured staff and trustees but without peer within the organization. Among the many interesting stresses of this position, which is inherently in conflict with both trustees and staff, is responsibility for both groups' performance. If either staff or trustees malfunction, it is frequently the director whose position is forfeited as a consequence. Although this is technically appropriate because it reflects the director's responsibility for both groups, it adds an ultimately uncontrollable factor to the work environment. The presence of too many factors beyond an individual's control is a primary cause of occupational stress with its deleterious effects upon general health and concentration.

A museum director, beset by economic insecurity and debilitating stress, may lack courage. The instinctive impulse for self-protection may dictate the wisdom of being less than assertive and not correcting inaccurate understandings of the museum's mission, goals, and objectives by either trustees or staff. Although any leader must select with care the issues on which to take a stand, the answers to questions of institutional mission and goals are not optional. Museum directors must be the leaders in their institutions. There is more to the title than the dictionary definition as one who manages, supervises, and regulates. Whether that person is called president or executive director, a museum director must provide direction for a museum, show everyone which way that institution is going, and lead the way. The director must lead first, and manage/supervise/regulate second, because the content and nature of the second duty are derived from the first. Of the standard list of questions—who, what, when, where, and why—the museum director's primary responsibility is to answer why. The response to *why* frequently answers *where* as both relate to rationale and direction. As these concerns are answered, the other questions more easily find answers. Clarity of interpretation, even more than consistency, must characterize the leadership of the director—the clear, translucent diamond within the organization.

Return to the geometric figure illustrating the director's position as the diamond link within a museum's human resources organization. The dimensions of the figure should now be sufficiently drawn to lift it multifaceted from the plane. A point faces you, pulling the figure, with a form not unlike that of the Concorde, into space. The top of the diamond in this three dimensional figure precedes it, just as the skilled and effective museum director leads the museum's trustees and staff. Where is that museum going? What is the nature of the space or void in which the figure travels?

Ah, in this field we have cleverly avoided that question with the complacent observation that each museum must set its own course and be evaluated not on its direction but on the appropriateness of procedures and policies to sustain momentum. The impact of that figure on the environment within which it exists—or the lack of impact—is not now, but only now, our concern. The social consequences of such autonomy may demand assessment in the coming decade. For the present it is sufficient to define the figure of the museum and the director as the diamond, the strong connecting link, within it—the diamond link that balances and directs the human resources which, in turn, animate and implement the museum's mission.

# 12

# The Director as Fiscal, Facilities, and Security Manager

by

Crawford Lincoln

CRAWFORD LINCOLN has been the president of Old Sturbridge Village in Massachusetts since 1978, prior to which time he spent a twenty-five-year career in the publishing business. He was awarded a B.A. by Yale University in 1950. The author of articles on museum management and a consultant to museums, he served for six years as a member of the Council of the American Association of Museums. He currently is a member of the AAM/ICOM board, has been a panelist for the National Endowment for the Humanities and the Institute of Museum Services, and is an examiner for the AAM Accreditation Commission.

The Richardson Parsonage at Old Sturbridge Village receives a coat of white paint as part of a continuous program of historic building maintenance. Courtesy of Chuck Kidd, Old Sturbridge Village, Sturbridge, Massachusetts.

s the several chapters of this book amply attest, there are probably as many different approaches to the job of running a museum as there are museums. My post carries the title of president rather than director, and I work for a large living history institution (full- and part-time staff of about six hundred, annual budget, approximately $10 million); but I believe there are some givens all museum leaders can relate to regardless of their institution's structure, focus, and size. I hope to demonstrate that museum leadership is not a science, but instead, an awesome and sometimes overpowering art.

We will be looking closely at fiscal, facilities, and security concerns the director must deal with. Let's start, however, with the basics. If directors are to be successful, they will need to approach their work with a deep sense of stewardship. They should have a clear understanding of the public trust that is ingrained in all aspects of a museum—its collections, its physical plant, its financial resources, its staff, its programs, and its heritage. Successful directors will bring to their work a highly visible personal integrity, and an unmistakable commitment to quality, and a sensitivity to the needs and aspirations of those colleagues who share the stewardship of the museum.

Individuals who are comfortable with change and eager to learn from others usually make first-rate museum directors and equally effective members of a support staff. To them, the mission statement is not a vaguely remembered summary of a bygone vision. Rather, it serves as a constant plumb line against which all of the institution's activities, programs, and resource allocations should be measured. Trouble may develop when the imperative of the mission statement is blurred by alluring, yet nongermane exhibition or accession opportunities. If the mission statement should be outdated or in need of refinement, the wise director will bring it to the attention of the trustees for action. After all, running a museum of whatever size is a complex task, and the reference point for one's efforts needs to be unmistakably clear. It's also a team effort! Curators, educators, researchers, and all others responsible for managing areas need to understand the mission.

All of the foregoing needs to be kept in mind as one deals with a museum's finances. In the simplest terms the museum director's job is to forward the mission of the museum within the framework of a balanced budget. Since an organization's resources are inevitably finite, one begins the process of building an operating budget by placing all of the possible revenue and expenditure options against the mission statement plumb line. Those that fail to measure up can be discarded, leaving those that remain to be sorted according to priority. The budgeting process is most successful when those responsible for expenditures and for generating receipts take an active role in budget formulation from the initial draft to the final document.

If all parties to the process have an understanding at the outset of the need to prioritize and work to build priorities within specific areas of responsibility against clearly defined institutional goals, the resulting document is sure to be a much more reliable and efficient guide to the museum's annual operation. Good teamwork up-front leads to better teamwork as the fiscal year unfolds.

Before presenting the final budget document to the trustees for approval, the director, however, must frequently step out of the role of chief staff advocate for its passage. A series of questions need to be answered *before* the numbers are inked in or passed through the word processor for the last time. Are the figures reasonable? How do they relate to the financial plan and experience of the previous year? What are the trends for the past several years, and how does next year's budget relate to them? If there are changes, how are they explained and justified? How realistic are the income projections? What are the factors that might adversely affect the anticipated results, and what kind of contingency or cushion should be planned for? What kind of monitoring should be in place to ensure adherence to the budget plan? How is the budget spread over the fiscal year, and what are the cash-flow projections? Have capital needs been detailed and are they presented with the operating budget package so the board will get the full picture?

At budget review time any of the foregoing questions may be raised by a financially savvy trustee, and the wise director will get the answers in place well before the session. To facilitate the review process, explanatory notes providing the answers can be attached to the packages. In any event trustees should be asked, at least once a year, how the budget package can be improved.

I'm a great believer in "no surprises management." This simply means that those who hold fiduciary responsibility for a given institution should be promptly advised of any significant deviations from a budget plan. In some cases this will be the entire board of trustees, in others, the executive committee or the finance committee and board chairperson. The director not only has an obligation to report the variance but should also provide recommendations for dealing with it. For example, living history museums have long been plagued by weather extremes, some of which can upset even the most conservative budget projections. And, frequently, contingency plans are not enough. In such cases a range of options can be prepared with recommendations for review by the appropriate board committee. If advice and counsel is sought early on by the director, the resulting board response, in many cases, can be a real lifesaver.

One of the most critical aspects of sound financial management is a well-thought-out plan for coverage and continuity in case the unexpected happens. What does a director do when the museum's treasurer, or chief bookkeeper, quits or dies? Or what happens if fire destroys the place where the museum's financial activity is centered? Or less ominously, how does the organization function when those who handle its finances take a two- or three-week vacation? The answer to these and other related questions one could raise should be worked out early on in a director's assumption of duties if the organization has no plans in place. Here is another area where knowledgeable trustees can provide valuable assistance from their own experience.

While the director need not be a master of fund accounting theory, it is essential that those to whom the books are entrusted are well versed in the subject. I am impressed when I learn of museums that are making it possible for accounting department personnel to attend seminars or take additional courses in their ever-changing field.

While check signing is not part of my daily routine, I do undertake the task, from time to time, to take the museum's financial pulse. I'm distressed when I find an instance where a cash discount, allowed by a vendor, has not been taken, and I make the effort to find out why so that a future lapse will not occur. A few dollars lost here and there cannot be retrieved and, over time, they do add up! And when placing an order it always pays to ask for a discount or a reduced price that recognizes the museum's nonprofit status.

If directors spent more time on controlling routine expenses, more of the museum's resources could be directed to paying adequate salaries, improving programs, and building collections. A review of the ten largest vendors in terms of a museum's disbursements is a good place to start. For example the monthly phone bill may suggest an opportunity to cut costs through the purchase of equipment to replace leased units. Perhaps a local foundation or corporate donor can be persuaded to provide the necessary funds. Heavy long-distance charges may indicate a need to utilize a WATS line or to undertake an economizing educational effort with staff. In some cases the acquisition, preferably by gift, of in-house printing equipment can reduce a major area of expense. Energy costs can often be reduced by pooling requirements with other nonprofits in the community and then putting the group's business out to bid. The bid process should be employed routinely for items, consultants, or projects estimated to exceed an agreed-upon amount. And if a board member's uncle is a significant supplier to the institution, good judgement and ethical standards suggest that regular bid procedures not be waived.

The important thing for museum directors and their trustees to remember is that they are stewards of a public trust and as such, they should always act on behalf of the public. Those who handle the museum's investments need to pay special attention to this point. Once portfolio objectives have been established by board or investment committee vote, the agent or individuals charged with carrying out those objectives should be held to the highest performance standards as measured annually by the basic indexes of the financial marketplace and the results of various professional fund managers. For those directors who are tempted to play the market by holding onto a stock gift to the museum, my advice is, *don't*. Stock gifts should always be referred immediately to the portfolio's duly appointed custodian for disposition. If all this sounds cumbersome, the donor can always be encouraged to sell the shares and deliver the proceeds of the sale instead.

Investment income is but one of many potential revenue streams that needs to be examined by today's museum director. Most museums and historical societies sell things in a shop or at a sales desk with the assumption that making money is at least one of the reasons for doing so. But how many directors really understand whether or not the sales are generating a profit or loss? If asked, whoever does a museum's books can usually provide an objective analysis of the profitability of its retail activity. And if the museum is fortunate to have a trustee with retail experience, valuable advice on pricing, turnover, inventory control, etc., is usually there for the asking. If the museum finds no appreciable return on its investment in shop merchandise, selling space, staff, and supplies, the continuance of the activity should be questioned, especially in the light of the mission statement discussed earlier.

A word is called for about membership programs. Does the museum exist to serve its members or does the membership exist to serve the museum? In my opinion the answer to this very simple question has far-reaching implications for the financial health of the institution. The director who answers, "Both" *may* be headed for trouble and the director who embraces the initial viewpoint, while rejecting the second, usually is already in financial trouble without quite knowing why.

It all gets back to the mission statement and the place it holds in the director's management outlook. Unless the time, energy, and resources invested in a membership program yield a *measurable* return on that investment beyond "good will," there will be a loss—a loss in services or programs for the public at large or an actual monetary loss—and a lost opportunity to strengthen the institution financially. If a membership operation contributes directly to the profit of an institution after deducting all related direct and indirect costs, then a member's unexpected bequest or major year-end gift can be viewed as a well-earned extra dividend.

In 1988 the Congress took a hard look at nonprofits' unrelated business income to see if present IRS guidelines are encouraging unfair competition with the profit sector, particularly small businesses. As of this writing no changes in the regulations have been adopted. Since the question has not been resolved, however, directors may wish to evaluate all income-producing activities of their institutions to see if they do, in fact, fall within the four corners of the mission statement and meet the test of being "substantially related" to the museum's purpose. Questionable areas need to be reviewed with professional counsel to ensure compliance with current law. Additionally, directors should consider lending their voices to the nonprofit chorus now defending the tax code exceptions which, for years, have been granted in recognition of contributions to the public good.

Finally, since we live in a litigious society, the prudent director will leave no stone unturned to ensure that the institution and its staff are in full compliance with all current federal, state, and municipal laws and regulations applicable to the museum's operation. Monetary judgments awarded for wrongful dismissal, sexual harassment, improper disposal of hazardous materials, violations of immigration or labor laws, etc., can have a devastating effect on an institution's financial stability. The director has an obligation to train the museum staff in their responsibilities to see that the law is obeyed in all matters touching their work. Here is another large area where trustees can provide solid advice drawn from experience in the world of work outside the museum. Directors take note—"I didn't know," and "I never dreamed it could happen here" are lame excuses for managerial incompetence. When was the last time you reviewed your museum's insurance coverage with your agent or risk management advisor?

As an introduction to my thoughts on the director's role as a manager of facilities, I will share with you a story about my late mother-in-law who spent her last years in a retirement home. One day, another resident of the home brought a visiting friend to my mother-in-law's room and said, "I want you to meet Mrs. Gulick; her son-in-law is the caretaker out at Old Sturbridge Village." As my mother-in-law told me this story with no little indignation in her voice, it occurred to me that *caretaker* was a particularly apt descriptor for much of a museum director's job and especially the work with buildings, or facilities as they're often called.

Those of us who work for a living history museum with various antique buildings, or for a historic house museum, are obliged to treat these structures in many ways as we would care for a fine piece of furniture or a valuable painting in the museum's collection. A museum's antique building is, after all, itself a part of the collection. It needs to be conserved and dealt with sensibly and realistically, particularly if it is to be occupied as a workplace or opened to streams of visitors.

Decisions relating to renovation, repair, and restoration of antique buildings often are best made with a team of professionals—researchers, educators, interpretive specialists, as well as maintenance and safety experts. Choices of materials and construction techniques, determinations of traffic patterns and interpretive scenarios, provisions for safety, lighting, fire suppression, and housekeeping equipment, and modifications required to conform to current regulations for handicapped access and emergency exits are appropriately shared with these qualified experts.

The input, up-front, of a practicing architect or registered engineer can frequently pay huge dividends to a cost-conscious director in addition to resolving some of the inevitable differences of opinion growing out of the specialized viewpoints of a museum's professional staff.

Most projects involving repair of old buildings take longer and cost more than originally planned on. Across America the number of projects delayed or disrupted by unforeseen construction problems is legion. All of the director's patience, tact, and creativity may be called upon to arrive at responsible solutions to difficulties. For obvious reasons considerations of responsible conservation and public safety will take precedence over the desirability of adhering to a published date for a re-opening gala.

New England winters have never been kind to old buildings and most directors in these parts plan on a springtime review of their institutions' property. A yearly checkup of facilities wherever located is mandatory, especially in light of today's concerns for safety in the workplace and the problem of public liability. I would add that failure to maintain a structure's exterior or interior appearance, while not a threat to public safety, can result in reduced attendance because of unnecessary unfavorable word-of-mouth publicity. As I see it a museum's entrance should, at all times, be one of its most attractive and inviting aspects.

Trade journals edited for building superintendents and groundskeepers are not part of the regular reading of most museum directors, nor should they be. From time to time, however, it helps to talk with those who are well informed on their subject matter so as to take advantage of the latest technology and materials in these highly specialized fields. Money saving is worthwhile in all areas of museum activity, and in the maintenance arena, it is essential.

As caretakers of the nation's cultural patrimony, museum directors have an enormous responsibility to see to its security. Escalating values of collections have encouraged thieves, both professional and amateur, to turn to museums where, in many instances, sad to say, the pickings are easy. Frequently the press reports on spectacular heists of paintings here and overseas, but often unpublicized are an increasing number of disappearances of smaller and less glamorous collection items such as teapots, inkwells, coins, etc. All this suggests that if security has been low on a museum director's priority list, there are compelling reasons to bring it to the forefront.

Eternal vigilance and occasional inconvenience are hallmarks of good museum security. I find it reassuring when I arrive at a locked door of a small historical society and read a notice advising that a tour is in progress and that someone will be along shortly to answer the bell. And when I'm on tour where the leader makes a point of corralling the stragglers before moving on, I know that the director has taken the time to see that the staff is well trained in security procedures. Locked doors, having to wait, and not being allowed to linger in unattended exhibit areas inevitably pose minor inconveniences for the museum visitor.

Today's security-conscious museum director has usually taken the process much further by instituting training for all staff, clarifying instructional philosophy regarding security, as well as restricting the distribution of keys to a few carefully screened personnel, and by limiting access to sensitive areas. Local law enforcement experts are often brought in to provide security instruction for staff. Risk management advisors are helping museums, large and small, upgrade their security practices. And in some parts of the country, the Smithsonian Institution has brought together individuals concerned with museum security to participate in seminars focused on problems of safeguarding collections from exterior and interior threats. A recent session on security issues, sponsored by the New England Museum Association in conjunction with the Smithsonian, was attended by directors of small museums as well as specialized staff from larger institutions. Those present agreed on the value of gathering periodically to keep pace with new developments in the field.

There is much to be said for the value of imagining one's self in a role other than that of a museum director. Viewing the institution through the eyes of a trustee can provide a new insight on the need for sound fiscal management. The outlook of the visitor can help a director identify those areas of deficiency in the museum's facilities that detract from the full enjoyment of the museum experience. And, if the director will take a few minutes to imagine how the collection might be ripped off, it is likely that previously unnoticed security shortcomings can be spotted.

In many ways today's museum director is like the leader of a college or university. The director needs to be ever-mindful of the calling and the import of the responsibilities that go with the title. New challenges need to be met with constructive solutions grounded in a deep commitment to public service and the mission of the institution.

The world of a museum, like that of a college, is a complex one and few loners are successful as their leaders. Even in very small museums there needs to be a group of caring and committed individuals working closely with the director to make the place work. Building that team can be one of the most rewarding aspects of the director's assignment. And with it all, there has to be a sense that the job is fun and the effort one makes is worthwhile. Most who have accepted the mantle of museum leadership would agree that this is so.

# 13
# The Director and the Public Sector

by

Martha Mitchell Bigelow

MARTHA MITCHELL BIGELOW recently retired as director of the Bureau of History of the Michigan Department of State, secretary of the Michigan Historical Commission, and State Historic Preservation Officer for Michigan, positions to which she was appointed in 1971. The earlier portion of her career was devoted to teaching at Mississippi College, Memphis State University, and the University of Mississippi. She was awarded her B.A. by the University of Montevallo, Montevallo, Alabama, and her M.A. and Ph.D. degrees by the University of Chicago. She served as vice president of AASLH from 1976–1978 and president from 1978–1980. She has published numerous articles about historical subjects and agencies.

Michigan State Capitol, Lansing, where gubernatorial and legislative decisions are made that impact on the Bureau of History of the Department of State and the Michigan Historical Commission. Courtesy of the John Curry Archives, State of Michigan, Lansing, Michigan.

*T*his discussion on the public sector and public policy is based on the author's experience in a publicly funded state agency. This director's experience differs from other directors in the Midwest whose agencies are largely historical societies that have a private sector as well as a public sector.[1] One assumes that challenges and opportunities are much the same; however, the reader should be aware that the examples used in this paper are from an agency funded entirely by state tax dollars.

Historical agencies funded solely or in part by public monies have traditionally faced a common dilemma of how to serve the public without losing their souls—that is without violating their dedication to sound history and professionalism. The fundamental role of the director in relation to the public sector is to maintain professionalism and sound history but be capable at the same time of juggling competing groups in order to find compromises that will be acceptable—if not pleasing—to each. Sometimes it is possible to find such a compromise; sometimes it is impossible. The director, however, in an agency subject to public pressure must be able to "pull off" such successful compromises the majority of the time or he will not long retain his position.

The competing groups with which the historical agency must deal are composed of many diverse interests. Among these are 1) the general public; 2) special interest groups including local historical organizations; 3) individual legislators; 4) the legislature as a whole; 5) the executive branch of the government, and; lastly, but not least, 6) the bureaucracy of which the agency is a part. The director must deal with all these constituencies. This requires a delicate tight-rope balancing act that seems always one misstep away from disaster.

Perhaps the best way to look at the director's role in a state agency is to examine each of these publics. In relation to the general public, the director must know the history of his state and region as well as that of the United States. He must keep abreast of the political, social, and economic trends in the nation and how they are reflected in his state. He must be able to lead his agency into new trends but must also know the attitudes of the people of his state well enough not to move too quickly. A case in point is changing public policy, or perceived public policy, on a national level and how that policy affects the states—for example, the Jimmy Carter administration's emphasis on minorities and the working class. Directives implementing these themes were sent to the states through all federal regulations but most particularly through the historic preservation programs and the grants made by the federally funded endowments.

The question for the director in cases like this is how far to take his agency in the direction of such a perceived national policy. Fortunately in the above instance, in the state of Michigan these themes fit the public consciousness of the people; however, in another state this might not have been the case. The director's decision to permit his agency to apply for grants and to develop exhibits and publications based on federal policy, shifts the direction of his agency for several years. He must be sure that his state wants to follow this plan and that he isn't just responding to a federal whim that will disappear with the next administration at the very time that his state agency projects are just beginning to come on line. The same situation exists in relation to changing administrations on a state level. The director must have the political acumen and the historical perspective necessary to know how to shift or not to shift his agency in relation to what he perceives as changing public policy as reflected in changing administrations.

The director must also always have in mind what he perceives to be policies that will be supported by the general public. Sometimes, however, it is very difficult to distinguish between special interest groups and the general public. Among special interest groups are historic preservationists, genealogists, local historians, planners, architects, city officials, legislators, and even competing groups within the agency itself. One of the best examples of the interplay of many of these diverse groups can be seen in the area of environmental review for historic preservation. For instance a project like preserving Tiger Stadium in Detroit brought pressure on the Bureau of History from the governor's office, the mayor's office of the city of Detroit, as well as other groups involved such as planners, architects, and engineers. Meanwhile the activists and preservationists brought pressure from the opposite point of view.

Sometimes in cases like this the agency's most ardent opponent has formerly been its most ardent supporter and vice versa. The director must be able to take with equanimity these shifting loyalties and always hold himself and his staff to the highest professional standards within his judgement of what is best from an overall point of view. It is only the director and his immediate staff that have information from all these competing elements. As a state agency looking at the general welfare rather than the special competing interests, the staff has the responsibility of looking at the overall picture and being as objective as it is possible to be. If this is done, it can defend its professional judgement with all groups.

Over the years, the agency, working with projects like those above, should build a reputation of integrity, honesty, and objectivity. It is crucial in the building of that reputation that the director see that a *process* of decision making is involved and that the process be documented. Every group must be aware that a decision is not the whim of one person but is the result of collective decision making of the entire historic preservation office or whatever section of the historical agency is involved in the current controversy. Only the director can see that this is the case, since the chain of command locates the power in his hands.

The necessity of having decision making be a documented process is particularly crucial in relationship to the legislature. Individual legislators often represent special interest groups. They are also the greatest potential supporters of the agency. As their constituents turn to them for support in regard to projects that they are interested in, the legislator has to turn to the agency and request that it take action. To be able to present to the legislator a documented process of decision making makes it much easier for him to reply intelligently to his constituents and support what you have done. This is particularly true in relationship not only to environmental review, but to programs such as state grants. When the bureau had a state grant program, the grants were scored on a numerical basis with certain criteria receiving a stated number of points. When a legislator's constituents appealed to him for redress when they had not received a grant, the legislator could point to the reason they had not done so and send them copies of the documented process. In no case did we have a legislator insist on any change being made when we were able to present this documentation.

As one looks at the agency in relationship to individual legislators, the director's attitude will be reflected right down the line throughout the agency. There is a tendency among staff to feel that politics interferes with professionalism. If this is accepted and emphasized by the director, the effect will be disastrous. The legislators consider any state agency to be at their beck and call. Consistent refusal to respond promptly and professionally will create an antagonistic atmosphere in the legislature that may be felt at appropriation time. The guidelines for working with the legislature set by the director of the Bureau of History in Michigan are as follows:

1. Answer all calls promptly and efficiently.
2. Within the framework of sound history and professionalism, provide the legislator with what he requests.
3. If you are unable to meet the legislator's requests, you must be able to show him why this is the case in a reasoned professional way. (The discussion of the grant program above is a case in point.)
4. Operate within the framework that what the legislator is requesting is what he thinks is best for his district and, therefore, is not politically motivated but arises from a concept of the general welfare for his particular area. Coming from that position, the staff member acts in a courteous and understanding way that disarms

the individual, whatever the outcome, even when it is contrary to what the legislator wants.

This director, operating from the above philosophical position, had only one incident in her entire eighteen years in office in which the bureau was threatened with a cut in appropriations because of an action it took in a legislator's district. A legislative aide, not the legislator himself, threatened this cut. This happened very early in her career when there was a controversy over Kaye Hall at Northern Michigan University in Marquette. The university wanted to tear down the National Register property, and as SHPO her office objected. The legislative aide, who assisted the Capitol Outlay Committee, remarked, "Don't you know that this legislator has charge of *your* budget?" The reply was, "Yes, I know that." There was no retaliation, however, because the legislator involved recognized that the director and her staff had acted objectively and professionally. During the years, as the Bureau's reputation for integrity and professionalism has grown, any tendency to make these kinds of threats seems to have disappeared.

Having just arrived on the scene from a university background, the above episode was very disillusioning. However, as the years have gone past, I have realized that it was naiveté that allowed me to be disillusioned. It has become more and more obvious to me that political science, as learned in schools of political science and historical administration, fails to properly equip individuals to function in the real world. As an aside, I would like to urge educators to adopt more realistic methods of teaching in these schools. Government courses are often taught in a vacuum totally removed from political practicality. Individuals, thus, coming into historical agencies from the universities are often frustrated in the reality that they see about them.

Students need to be more aware that our political system is based on compromise and that compromise is not a dirty word. Compromise is a system that operates so that you get something and I get something, and nobody gets everything. It isn't pretty and it's sometimes messy, but it stumbles along and it works. If one insists on being absolutely right, there is no area for compromise and the system will not succeed. There is a danger, of course, that compromise may become a way of life, and obviously there is a point beyond which compromise should not be made. In a historical agency that point must always be sound history and professionalism. However, that does not prevent the historical administrator from honoring the integrity, desire for service, and interest in the common good that underlie what may appear to be political requests from legislators. If an attitude like this is taken, the agency will develop over the years a rapport with the legislature that will be exceedingly valuable.

An example of the interweaving of special interest and the interest of the general public exists for this director in her relationship to a small museum built by the bureau in Negaunee, a small community in the Upper Peninsula of Michigan. Representative Dominic Jacobetti from that area supported a group of his constituents who were trying to establish a museum at the Carp River Forge, the site where the first iron was manufactured in Michigan's great iron range. There was no question in the director's mind about the importance of the site despite its isolated location. She chose to work with this small group of people and Representative Jacobetti in securing the museum. The director became involved in 1972. The county and the group organized to create the museum gave the historic site to the bureau. The representative who was on the appropriations committee kept putting money in the bureau budget in odd places to accomplish the museum step by step.

Our first step was to survey and get the land ready, and second to build a parking lot. Representative Jacobetti then put the money in the Capital Outlay to build the building. The state was in economic recession and Governor William Milliken vetoed the appropriation. It looked as though the bureau might be embarrassed by ending up with just a parking lot in the wilderness, but no one gave up! In the meantime the representative became chairman of the Appropriations Committee, and a compromise was reached between the chairman and the governor. The money was provided, and the building built and dedicated during Michigan's Sesquicentennial in 1987. The whole process took fifteen years! The question, of course, is—was this just a special interest or was it for the public good? To the director it seemed to be both because of the importance of the iron industry and the site to Michigan history.

In the long run the actions outlined above, in the director's eyes, worked to benefit tremendously the cause of history in the state and to advance the public interest. I, most certainly, did not know that the bureau would later benefit so greatly from the above action. The major effort of the present administration in Michigan has been to acquire for the agency a new building in Lansing that would permit the bureau to adequately exhibit the rich history of the state. In the last four years that has been accomplished; however, in order to have outstanding, interpretive exhibits more money was needed even though in the money appropriated for the building, $2.5 million was designated for exhibits. Members of the Department of State and the director lobbied the legislature for an extra $2.5 million. The appropriation passed easily in the House where Representative Jacobetti shepherded it through his committee. It ran into trouble in the Senate.

The day it was to come before the Senate Appropriations Committee, I expected to testify and was flying back from Negaunee where I had been working on the Carp River Forge Museum. I was "fogged in" at the airport. I called Representative Jacobetti's office and told them where I was and asked if the representative could do something to help me. Representative Jacobetti himself went to the Senate Committee and personally pleaded the bureau's case. He told the Senate Committee that "This is the first time I have lobbied for something that wasn't in the Upper Peninsula." The Senate voted the money. When I got back to Lansing one of the members of the Senate Committee said jokingly, "Martha, had I known you were from the Upper Peninsula, I would never have opposed it in the first place."

Without Representative Jacobetti's support, I am convinced that the bureau never would have gotten the money for the exhibits that will benefit school children, thousands of Michigan citizens, and the cause of history generally. Was this logrolling? Was this politics? Was this a special interest? Was this the interest of general public? To me it appears to be all of those; but I believe that working with the legislators and honoring their dignity and integrity, while always maintaining one's own values, develops mutual trust and respect so that all the small welfares will come together into the general welfare—which in the director's mind, of course, is the advancement of the bureau's purposes. That purpose as stated in our planning document is:

> The Bureau of History is the official state agency for historical programs and activities that are the responsibility of the State of Michigan. The purpose of the Bureau is to preserve, protect, chronicle, interpret, and present the history of Michigan to its people and visitors. This is accomplished on both a state and local level through museum, archival, and archaeological programs, historic preservation, publications, and research.

To this director, working to advance the cause of history in outlying areas is a major part of that purpose, and only by providing help in local districts can one expect support from the legislature for the agency's overall program.

It is important to note, however, that rapport with individual legislators does not always translate into rapport with the legislature as a whole. When the legislature sits as a body working on the appropriation process, it is swayed by many demands outside of its ordinary way of operation. For instance, the target budget set by the governor will often necessitate cuts that many of the legislators would personally prefer not to make. They also face increasing demands from those lobbying for prisons, mental health, and welfare—causes that always take precedence over cultural activities. It has been my experience in the legislative process that only in very rare circumstances of overall prosperity is it possible for the cultural agencies of the state to make any kind of sizeable gain. Over a series of years, however, slight gains here and there mount up and they are achieved largely through personal relationships with individual legislators.

As one looks at the overall funding process for appropriations for a public historical agency, one wonders how the agency ever makes gains at all. The steps through which the director has to go are complicated and at each step one can win or lose. The first step is to persuade the department of which you are a part to forward your request to the governor. The Bureau of History is in the Department of State and until the last year or so, our requests were considered relatively unimportant compared with the many millions of dollars the department requested for other programs. It is the director who must convince the officials of the department of the importance of his program and the necessity to expand its activities to reach more of the public.

Once the department has agreed to support that request, the Program Revision Request (as it is termed) is forwarded to the Department of Management and Budget (DMB) which operates directly under the governor. DMB then considers that request in light of the governor's priorities, the overall budget constraints, and sometimes the personal predilections of the budget analysts themselves. If the proposed program change gets past this hurdle, it then goes to the legislature. Here the agency's relationships with the legislature come into play, but the Department of State still has the determining role.

In the budget process, if the department does not lobby vigorously for that element of the program that the historical agency is seeking, it will be the first item cut as the legislature tries to balance the state budget (a balanced budget is mandated by the Michigan Constitution). Unfortunately for this director, she did not have the opportunity to lobby directly with the legislature as do the directors of historical societies like those of Minnesota, Wisconsin, and Ohio. The Department of State of which the bureau is a part has designated legislative liaisons and the department prefers that lobbying be left to it. Thus in Michigan the role of the department in the legislative process is more important than it is in other states of the Midwest.

If the proposed program expansion passes all the above hurdles, is approved by the legislature, and not vetoed by the governor, then the process of putting it into effect brings into play the general public, or perhaps one should say a general public made up of many competing special interests—the public constituencies of the agency. The director cannot consistently ask the legislature for increased program expansions for only one area. If, for instance, year after year he favors the museums or historic sites to the detriment of the archives, publications, or archaeology, outrage will be expressed not only by his staff but by the public which supports the archives or historic preservation or whatever area is perceived as being neglected.

The director thus faces competing constituencies within his own agency. However, the eagerness of staff members to push their own area is usually a demonstration of their devotion to their profession, and in a historical agency it is crucial that the staff have that attitude. Unlike the universities where the scholar receives recognition because of his individual work, it is the team effort in a historical agency that makes the difference. If the individual is unable to subordinate his individual efforts to the good of the whole, the publication, the exhibit, or the preservation project will not get done or, at least, not well. Job satisfaction, therefore, comes from a sense of community and devotion to the profession. It is important that the director recognize and nurture that devotion even when it causes him problems. It is out of these competing devotions that an excellent historical agency develops. What the director hopes to see happen is perhaps best summed up by Larry Tise in an article in *The Public Historian.* Tise wrote:

> The sooner we learn that each such institution operates in society as a corporate entity with a life and memory of its own to promote, interpret, and preserve our past, that such entities must be nurtured up and sustained in ways not reproductible in the history classrooms, and *the historians must be willing to subsume their own personalities and whims in order to build such institutions,* the sooner we will be able to find a proper relationship between history, historians and the [public] history needs of American society and government.[2]

The director plays a key role in creating this atmosphere. He accomplishes this by extending appreciation to his staff members for their teamwork and professionalism, and by attaining a reputation for being fair to all segments of the historical profession represented in his agency.

In regard to getting legislation passed that is favorable to the agency, in Michigan the Department of State again plays the key role. The legislation is drafted at the request of the bureau, but after that the department takes over the process. One would assume in the other private/public agencies that the director would approach a friendly legislator with a proposed bill in order to start the process. For both types of agencies, however, the passage of the bill depends on the agency's relationship to the members of the legislature and its grassroots historical compatriots. In the final analysis it is the small and large historical societies and museums, as well as history buffs throughout the state, who, by lobbying their own legislators, can get a bill through the legislature for the state agency. Few historical program bills will be successful without local grassroots support.

This paper has not spoken much about grassroots support; however, the many small museums and historical societies are always there in the back of the director's mind, as their welfare is the welfare of history in the state. The destiny of the state agency and theirs is intertwined. They are not only one's support in the legislature but also in the job one does. Being a director is probably the most challenging job in the public history field. These challenges or problems are exciting and this director, as she reflects on the end of her public service, wishes only that she had gotten into historical agency work sooner. As much as she loved university teaching, it doesn't compare with the excitement and challenges of having your fingers on the heartbeat and pulse of a great state's historical development.

Unfortunately often the job is filled with headaches, frustrations, and pettiness. However, for a built-in safety valve, the director would get in her car and head out to speak to or just visit with the local historical societies, museums, and other local historical groups. These areas outside of the Capitol, soothed her when she was upset with their appreciation of her coming and of everything done for them. They themselves were so dedicated and produced such marvelous results with so few resources—other than the most important ones of interest, enthusiasm, and dedicated volunteerism—that she marveled at their accomplishments and returned to Lansing renewed and rejuvenated, ready to join battle and to fight another day for the cause of history in Michigan!

# 14

# African American Museums and the New Century: Challenges in Leadership

by

Amina J. Dickerson

AMINA J. DICKERSON is director of education and public programs at the Chicago Historical Society. She served as president of the DuSable Museum of African American History in Chicago from 1985 to 1989. Her previous museum affiliations include the Afro-American Historical and Cultural Museum in Philadelphia and the National Museum of African Art at the Smithsonian Institution in Washington, D.C. She has also served as a consultant on Afro-American museums, exhibition development, and arts organizations. She holds an M.A. in Arts Management from American University in Washington. Over the years she has lectured widely and made numerous professional presentations. Currently, she is on the board of directors of the African American Museums Association and the council of AASLH.

Entrance to the DuSable Museum of African American History, Chicago, Illinois. The museum was established by Margaret Burroughs and six colleagues in 1961 as the Ebony Museum of History and Art. Courtesy of the DuSable Museum of African American History, Chicago, Illinois.

Alarge number of research libraries, archives, historical societies, genealogy groups, and black museums share the common purpose of collecting and preserving material on
history and cultural heritage of African Americans. Their mission is to
provide a more accurate picture of a history that has been continually,
and in many instances purposefully, neglected over time. Since the establishment of the College Museum at Hampton Institute in 1868, some 150
institutions in thirty-seven states have furthered this mission, operating
against considerable odds to document the story of the African presence
worldwide.

Historically the social and economic condition of black Americans
(the primary audience of these museums) has limited the scope of the resources with which black institutions operate. The absence of sufficient
resources has often adversely affected the patterns of organizational development of African American museums. Yet, despite such obstacles,
these institutions have created a bond with the public and filled a void
within the larger realm of museums and historical organizations in the
country, and the evolution of such institutions on the whole has been
successful and has in itself a rich history. This essay briefly examines aspects of the history of African American museums as well as some of the
organizational challenges their leaders will face in preparing for the
new century.

## The Emergence of African American Museums

The role of museums in the cultural, social, and political development of African Americans is significant and varies from other Americans as a result of the unique slavery-derived experience of blacks in this
country over a period of four hundred years. Unlike most Americans the
majority of blacks in the United States did not voluntarily migrate to this
country.

Bettye Collier–Thomas, historian and director of the Bethune
Museum and the Archives of Black Women's History in Washington,
D.C., has observed that

> . . . museums, churches, courts, and other vital societal institutions
> do not function apart from the larger society. They mirror the
> thoughts, practices, and beliefs of the dominant racial and cultural
> group. . . . Thus, a society that defines a given group as inferior is un-
> able to give positive recognition to individual or group achievements.[1]

Black museums reflect black heritage and are created out of a specific
need to "define black achievements, to celebrate their blackness, and to

honor individual black contributions."[2] According to historian John Hope Franklin, this "search for authority" in the presentation by African Americans of their history began in earnest during the late nineteenth century when a number of black historical societies were established.

Beginning with the Bethel Literary and Historical Association (c. 1880), the American Negro Historical Society (1887), and following the turn of the century, the Negro Society for Historical Research, the activities sponsored by these organizations were, in many ways, precursors to African American museums.[3] The College Museum in Hampton, Virginia, was founded in 1868 to "enrich the vocational and academic instruction of the student body while providing otherwise unavailable cultural experiences for a broader community."[4] The first formally organized black museum, it secured a distinguished collection that contained important African art works acquired by a black nineteenth-century missionary to Africa, a significant collection of Native American Indian material acquired between 1878 and 1920, and important works of contemporary African American art including a major bequest from the Harmon Foundation.[5]

Other early museums were fortunate beneficiaries of collections lovingly developed by bibliophiles and lay students of history. One pioneering collector was Arthur Alfonso Schomburg, a black Puerto Rican immigrant to New York. Told in school that "the Negro has no history," Schomburg embarked upon a lifelong quest for information about Africans and their descendants throughout the world. He began serious collecting in 1910 and developed diverse holdings of manuscripts, rare books, pamphlets, sheet music, and art works. By 1926 the magnitude of the collection led to its purchase by the Carnegie Foundation for the Harlem branch of the New York Public Library. The Schomburg Center is today considered the foremost research facility of its kind in the world, with holdings in excess of five million items detailing the histories of blacks in Africa, the Americas, and elsewhere in the world.[6]

The 1920s "encouraged racial pride, a continuing interest in the civilizations of black Africa, and a redefining of the meaning of the black experience in America."[7] On the campuses of historically black colleges, museums were seen as vehicles to enhance teaching and education generally for the academic community; since the late 1920s their collections have been widely used by students, faculty, and often, the community as well. In addition to Howard University (Washington, D.C.), there are important collections at Fisk (Tennessee), Lincoln (Pennsylvania), Tuskegee (Alabama), Bennett (North Carolina), Morgan State (Baltimore), and Talladega (Florida) universities.[8] If it were not for their efforts, much visual art work by African American artists as well as important historical documents would have been dispersed or perhaps lost.

## The Impact of the Civil Rights Movement

Despite advances in the cultural arena during the 1940s and 1950s, the racial and political climate in the United States remained basically unchanged. Popular involvement with civil rights activities prompted a new imperative in black history. As historian Vincent Harding notes:

> . . . since the 1950s is inextricably and dialectically tied to the resurgence of our people's struggle for freedom in that same period. In other words, our post–1955 freedom movement created the major setting and stimulus for the newest coming of black history. . . . The power behind and within the resurgence has been primarily the power of our people to define themselves, their future, and their understanding of their past.[9]

Within this climate, the San Francisco Afro-American Historical and Cultural Society was founded in 1955 through the combined efforts of a historical association and a literary society. The collection includes art, books, periodicals, and many valuable photographs.

In Chicago, Margaret Burroughs continued work in cultural education that she had started in the 1930s with the South Side Community Art Center. With six colleagues she formed the Ebony Museum of History and Art in 1961, now the DuSable Museum of African American History. Dr. Charles Wright established the Afro-American Museum of Detroit in 1965. Other museums founded during this era included the Amistad Research Center, originally at Fisk University in Tennessee and later relocated to New Orleans, and the Society for the Preservation of Historic Weeksville, an all-black community located in what is now Brooklyn. Similar efforts also took place in New York, Connecticut, and Rhode Island.

In 1967 the Anacostia Neighborhood Museum was established as a bureau of the Smithsonian Institution. Conceived as an "outpost" of the main Smithsonian complex in Washington, D.C., it instantly became a model for museum outreach, its goal to "enliven the community and enlighten the people it serves."[10] The museum received funding and technical support from the Smithsonian, but the planning and daily administration were controlled by the community. Other efforts during this era were directed exclusively to the preservation of black visual arts, though for the majority of African American museums both history and art serve as the focus of collections.

The Museum of Afro-American History, founded at Boston in the early 1970s, was instrumental in the restoration of the African Meeting House, "the oldest existing black church building still standing in the United States." With the meeting house as the centerpiece, the museum developed a walking tour called the "Black Heritage Trail," which explores fourteen important sites in the history of Boston's nineteenth-century black community.[11]

The Civil Rights Movement created a new black cultural renaissance. In their expression of a black perspective and through their efforts to preserve and present black history, these museums provided a "way of empowerment" and moved awareness of African American history to a new plateau. Joy Ford Austin, a museum consultant and former director of the African American Museums Association (AAMA), suggests that black museums "may be the spiritual and educational bridge that black colleges and churches can't be for everybody."[12] The large number of these museums that emerged during the late 1960s and early 1970s supports this thesis. Some, such as the museums in Philadelphia and in California, benefit from government funding that was available during the observance of the nation's bicentennial. Others were formed with far fewer resources, inspired simply by the awareness that emerged from the movement. Between 1975 and 1985 black museums were formed in California, Texas, South Carolina, Oklahoma, Nebraska, Colorado, Georgia, and Virginia; they called upon the experiences of those previously established to assist them in their development. As a result greater sophistication in exhibition and facilities design, fiscal management, staff training, and strong research activity were evident from the beginning.

In more than a century of growth and development, nearly 150 new institutions have joined the ranks of the pioneering College Museum at Hampton. All are essentially united by a single mission—"responding to the need to define ourselves."[13] As John Kinard, the former director of the Anacostia Neighborhood Museum, summarized in an article in *American Visions* magazine:

> Those that have lasted and those that are coming on stream are responding to a modern-day imperative. Blacks sense the need to complete their life cycle. For a long time, education was our main kingdom. Then the political kingdom, then the social. Now it is the cultural kingdom. Culture embraces religions, lifestyle, heritage, and all the questions that have to be with being.[14]

By their sheer number and rapid growth, it is evident that African American museums fill a void that is perceived by the public. These institutions forge a link between history and tradition, continuity and change, past and future.

## Challenges in Institutional Development

An African American museum places great importance on its relationship with its audience. Barry Gaither, a pioneer in black museum work, often speaks passionately about the responsibility of these institutions to their communities:

> The community gives us our legitimacy . . . [our] presence informs and reforms [our] neighborhoods. . . . We are building our institutions in the black community, and they belong to that community.[15]

In many cases the museum also services as a community or cultural center; its rationale embodies the traditional standards of service and education that are at the very heart of the work that black museums do. In defining their mission black museums often seek to serve the broadest possible mandate for their communities—educative, social, political, and civic. The challenge is in achieving professional goals without sacrificing the spirit and soul of the institution. Needing flexibility, their mission statements have purposely been general and philosophical in nature. During the early stages of development in black museums, less focus was given to the conceptual, temporal, and geographic parameters of an institution's collections. Existing statements have included such language as "sharing contributions and information about black achievements."

In the formative years many of the museums felt compelled to examine the full picture of black history—locally, nationally and internationally. The global approach resulted directly from the void in available information and the complexity of the subject itself, beginning with a vast African ancestry. Such overly broad mission statements made it difficult to balance and prioritize community needs with those of collection, preservation, and exhibition development. In recognition of this, recently formed museums have explicit statements that clearly establish institutional responsibility to collect, preserve, and interpret the history and art of African Americans. The older museums are reviewing and refining their missions in more specific language, a move certain to help in decisions of resource allocation for the needs of the various collections.

African-American museums might collectively examine along national lines ways in which reshaping their respective missions can stimulate a comprehensive approach to the documentation and collection of black history and culture throughout the country. Certainly the substantial increase in the number of these museums suggests that it may be time to reevaluate mission statements. Since no single institution needs to tell the "whole story" they now can give greater attention to regional or local history and art, placing such efforts in the larger historical picture of the African diaspora worldwide.

In similar fashion, a comparison of missions may reveal gaps in available scholarship for significant aspects of regional or local black history and could encourage greater institutional collaboration in acquiring

and sharing collections. Such cooperation allows a director more lati-
tude in allocating limited resources. It may also help identify areas that
are worthy of specialized emphasis; the Black American West Museum
in Denver, Colorado, for example, concentrates on the experiences of
black cowboys and pioneers in the settlement of the West. Such specialization can help create stronger relationships between the museum and
local communities. Ultimately the museum seeks to create a broader
awareness of the African American experience while it contributes to
scholarship and the profession. It is the role of the director to set the
course for this effort by creating a delicate balance between public service and research initiatives, all of which begins with a concise, clearly
focused statement of mission. His challenge is to work with his board of
trustees to construct a thoughtful statement which sets parameters
within a fertile interpretive scope.

## The Impact of the Mission Statement on Collections Development

A further consequence of the mission statement is the imperative it
suggests for the collections policy. A 1987 study of black museums conducted by the AAMA, noted that nearly 42 percent of the responding
museums (fifty-two museums in twenty-three states and Canada) indicated that they are history museums. Others identified themselves as ethnic cultural centers (19 percent), art museums (15 percent), or historic
houses or sites (13 percent). This indicates a broad scope for the development of permanent collections.

In his article "Afro-Americana: Defining It, Finding It, and Collecting
It," Byron Rushing explores a series of considerations in collecting materials about the black experience, including "philosophical and ideological
questions" such as a definition of "Afro-American" [and now African
American] and its relationship to blacks in the Americas and in Africa.[16]
These questions must be answered in order to determine an appropriate
acquisitions policy for museums, for the answers will determine much
about the objects the institution should seek to acquire. In developing
collections both black art and history museums face tremendous challenges because of limited funds available for acquisitions, costs related to
providing appropriate care and conservation, and the rising expense of
mounting quality exhibitions. To a certain extent many objects and
works of art relevant to these institutions have already been acquired by
larger museums that are "content to own and not display." Frequently,
however, many materials have not yet been collected and languish in the
basements and attics of community residents. The challenge for museum leadership is to identify and collect such materials; doing so also

provides an opportunity to develop greater rapport with target audiences.

At the Afro-American Historical and Cultural Museum (AAHCM) in Philadelphia and a few other institutions around the country, new methods are being employed to expand collections with the assistance of the community. The approach, used by Rowena Stewart at both the AAHCM and earlier at the Rhode Island Black Heritage Society, utilizes the knowledge and experience inherent in the black community. A team consisting of a historian, a community representative, the museum curator, and, possibly, an education staff member makes public its interest in identifying and locating specific materials for purposes of research and exhibition through press releases, radio and television announcements, correspondence, and meetings with community organizations and church groups. These "calls-for-objects" are usually directed to a specific theme or planned exhibition. The team collects materials through community forums, home visits, and oral interviews. Scholars then work with the community to secure adequate documentation and validation of the objects. Interpretive materials and programs are developed, and permanent records of the objects can result from their use in an exhibition, publication, or catalog. During the exhibition, community volunteers continue to work with the museum as docents and tour guides.[17]

The process, which has been used in mainstream institutions as well as specialized museums, imbues in participants a sense of the importance and value of personal objects to the history of black people and, in many instances, leads to gifts or bequests to the museum. In giving objects to the museum, the community sees itself as an extension of that history and is likely to take more active involvement because of the interest it now has in the museum. For their part both the scholars and the museum can pride themselves on the research accomplished and the identification of objects by which the collections are enhanced, both artifactually and in documentary data.

Sometimes the team and community process focuses only on identification of the objects and their short-term use in exhibitions. The Afro-American Family History Project, headed by Carole Merritt, used that approach for a research/exhibition project in the early 1980s. It determined that the materials would best be preserved by remaining with their owners. "These are the personal legacies of families," observed Merritt, "and they should not be asked to give up their family heirlooms unless they are strongly inclined to do so."[18]

## Collections Management and Development

Management of collections represents *the* major challenge facing directors of African American museums. For at least 52 percent of the respondents in the AAMA survey, collection documentation was inadequate. Collection policies did not exist for 56 percent of the museums, nor did they cover loans (58 percent) or the disposal (or deaccession) of objects (71 percent). These findings suggest a serious need for more aggressive oversight of collections by trustees and staff, particularly since this area is critically important to the attainment of AAM accreditation, which 54 percent of the museums stated they intend to seek.[19] The survey identified a checklist of curatorial needs to be addressed to ensure that the cultural patrimony of African Americans is not lost through deterioration or misuse.

In addition to the need for detailed collection policies, many museums had only limited information on their holdings and need both inventories and catalog data. Very few have conservation programs, as black museums can rarely afford to have a staff conservator. The absence of current inventories makes it difficult to assess the breadth of available materials documenting the black experience and limits research and collection-sharing opportunities among institutions. Without such information on collections, it is difficult to develop "an active, deliberate, and analytic policy for collecting the contemporary."[20]

Black museums appear to be acutely aware of the many challenges they face regarding collections management. To help familiarize trustees with the policies and issues related to collection, self-study programs and board development sessions are used with increasing frequency. The AAMA survey recommends that training and assistance be given to black museums to ensure that proper registration, inventory, and cataloging methods are conducted. Counsel is also needed in the preparation of comprehensive collection policies that will, in turn, set forth guidelines for collection management. The survey further suggests that AAMA

> . . . find financial assistance to provide training and other support for a general program of inventorying and cataloging of collections; and to assist black museums in making others aware of their collections for the purposes of research.[21]

AAMA is also to spearhead an effort to secure financial support for a national survey of collections. As for training opportunities, African American museum directors should seek involvement from the broader community of museums to collaborate with them to provide ongoing, in-house training and internships. Commensurate effort is needed with university museum studies programs jointly to recruit and train aspiring black and other minority professionals. Such a pool of talent will eventually serve not only African American museums but the larger museum community concerned with affirmative action issues as well.

With regard to future acquisitions, limited funds will make it difficult for African American museums to purchase new artifacts. Consequently, black museum leaders will have to increase efforts to obtain gifts and donations of artifacts. The process utilized at AAHCM is a dynamic approach to collecting materials that can be followed in other institutions around the country. Cooperative efforts among black and other museums can well be made to promote nationally the need for gifts or in regional efforts to collect materials that can be owned in common by two or more museums. As the new century approaches, collections management, documentation, and acquisition of objects and artifacts that are representative of contemporary black culture will be priorities for many directors and trustees guiding African American museums.

## Education in Black Museums

The role of education in all museums has taken on added prominence in the last two decades and has contributed greatly to their rising popularity. Yet within the field there is still much debate about what constitutes museum education and how learning is facilitated. The AAM report observes that "although museums are plainly institutions of object-centered learning and there is interest among educators and administrators alike in formulating museum learning theory more clearly, there is no accepted philosophical framework."[22] A consensus still does not exist on what constitutes learning in the context of museums.

In this climate, education in African American museums largely parallels what is occurring in the broader field. Tours for school groups, lectures and workshops, the performing arts, and special events are sponsored in nearly all black museums. They also have struggled with the issue of how visitors learn in their institutions. For directors and their education staff the challenge is complicated by lack of demographic information about visitors to black museums. Of the countless studies that have been conducted over the years on museum visitation, no known work has been done on visitor behavior in black museums. Similarly, the AAMA survey revealed that most of these museums "do not have accurate data on their visitors." Based on the "guestimates" provided in the study, the largest number of visitors to these museums were African Americans, but it is obvious that black museums need to gather more detailed information about visitors through evaluations and surveys. Progress in collection documentation will benefit education as well, providing substantive information needed to develop interpretive activities. Perhaps this effort can begin by assessing the educational content of existing programs to determine their strengths and weaknesses.

Zora Felton, curator of education at the Anacostia Museum and an innovator in museum education programs for African American audiences, encourages black museum leaders to consider an approach that will acknowledge the needs of black youth and "that recognizes strengths, abilities, and culture and incorporates them into (the) learning process . . . building a curriculum that will provide for holistic learning, group learning, informal environments, a spirit of social consciousness, a strong self-concept, and a knowledge of black history and culture."[23]

In 1986 the AAMA appointed a special Education Commission to review museum education in black museums and to respond "to an often-expressed need of (AAMA) members for their staff and volunteers to be aware of the purposes and practices of education in museums as well as the general issues impacting African American life and culture."[24] Through this commission, the AAMA may well organize a full-scale research effort on issues such as audience experience, utilization of research results in exhibition design and in development of interpretive materials and programs, and the role of academic research. In the interim the range of educational services and docent-aided gallery programs is growing in these museums, with strong encouragement of the public.

## Staffing

The first generation of black museum leaders entered the field from a variety of occupations. Margaret Burroughs of Chicago received training as an artist and educator, Charles Wright of Detroit as a physician, and others in the fields of the humanities, social work, and community service. They usually learned on the job rather than through formal museum studies programs. With few exceptions opportunities for blacks to work in museums were limited to African American museums until the post–civil rights era of the late sixties to mid-seventies. As the number of black museums increased, the need for trained personnel grew as well, despite the limited availability of trained black professionals and insufficient funds to hire talented individuals. The AAMA study also indicated a need for continued training for existing staff in addition to aggressive recruitment and training for entering professionals. Nearly 44 percent of the responding museums cited a desire for ongoing staff training in areas that included museum management, conservation, preservation, documentation, and exhibition design.

Black museums do avail themselves of training offered by the Smithsonian Institution, the African American Museums Association, and the American Association for State and Local History, among others. The specific experience gaps of these museums, however, suggest the need for specialized programs to enable staff to develop greater expertise while continuing work within their institutions.

## Funding and Fiscal Stability

Nearly all prospects for organizational growth within African American museums necessitate the potential for increased monetary resources. Thus, fund raising was first on the list of needs cited by directors in the AAMA survey. The steadily increasing number of black museums has resulted in greater competition for dollars. This, in turn, has resulted in more aggressive efforts to develop new fund-raising strategies. John Kinard, in an address to the AAMA in 1980, stated, "It is clear to us now that we must have a massive infusion of funds into this family of institutions or they will not survive."

With the specter of reduced budgets in government arts and humanities programs, smaller corporate and private donations as a result of mergers, takeovers, and changes in the tax laws, and an uncertain financial climate affecting the investment portfolios of foundations, financial stability continues to be one of the most important concerns of black museums. Effective fund raising requires ongoing research and cultivation, which is generally difficult for directors faced with the limited staff size that is the norm within these institutions.

Reliance upon government funding is a short-term solution, for once those funds dry up, as history has shown, an institution finds it very difficult to replace them, with a resulting negative impact on operations. The outcome of applications to the National Endowment for the Arts or the Humanities or to the Institute for Museum Services is unpredictable, and the levels of funding are often disappointingly low. Grants awarded are usually for special programs and cover only a small percentage of operating expenses.

In response African American museums are striving to create diversified funding sources and to capture private dollars. Membership campaigns are being waged with increased sophistication, incorporating direct-mail efforts as well as telemarketing and person-to-person appeals. While these are not new strategies, inadequate finances have caused them to be more slowly implemented in African American museums. More museum leaders are establishing annual fund campaigns and seeking special gifts and bequests as they attempt to develop a broader base of individual donors. Deferred giving, becoming popular with black universities, is not yet pursued by most black museums, though the long-term benefits are attracting more interest than ever before. Endowments are almost unknown in the black museum community but need to be explored. Earned income initiatives, such as gift shop sales, are another increasingly important source of revenue, as are special fund-raising benefit events. Finally, the entrepreneurial effort within black museums to develop specialized products based on their collections represents another opportunity.

Thus, strong fund-raising campaigns, launched with the full support of boards of trustees, and increased efforts to secure contributions from a variety of sources require an ever-higher percentage of time in a director's already demanding schedule. Yet implementing such strategies is critical for the long-term survival of these museums, since it will take much more than the current levels of federal and state funding to ensure the ongoing growth, professional development, and long-term independence of African American museums.

## The Role of the Board of Trustees

The traditional profile of a museum trustee in mainstream institutions is of an individual who has achieved a high level of business or professional success, is well-off financially, commands prestige within the community, and often has cultivated a specialized knowledge of the area of collection for which the museum is known. Within African American museums, trustees more often are individuals recognized for their community leadership or activism. They are primarily concerned with service to the community and the development of programs that reflect the interests and needs of local residents. "Our trustees come to museums from various occupations and with various talents but are united in their desire to improve the lives of people in their community."[25] Often their personal financial resources and experience with museums is limited. Their work with black museums stems from their commitment to the teaching of black history and the development of black institutions in the community.

The museums founded in the early 1960s and 1970s grew out of the vision of a *principal founder* who provided not only the leadership, but oftentimes the financing and manpower as well. Board members were frequently the founder's friends, family members, and associates. That structure serves institutional needs in the beginning but may impede growth and stability at a later period as the duties of trustees increase. Thus, an important aspect of the board's role is its responsibility to plan for succession, both on the board and in the leadership of the institution. Policies of board rotation should be enforced to ensure that new ideas and skills are incorporated to guide the institution's development, and there should be a long-term plan to address the needs of the institution and the inevitable changes in leadership. Considering the special requirements and perspectives of African American museums, such planning may prove to be one of the most important roles for the board as an institution prepares now for the second generation of leadership. Failure to plan for transition may lead to internal disruption, apprehension among staff members, and uncertainty on the part of the public and actual or possible funders. A well-managed transition provides an opportunity for an institution to position itself to implement new goals, revitalize programs, evaluate progress, and plan for the future. It can effectively demonstrate organizational growth and stability to the public.

Another important aspect of trusteeship is the responsibility for fundraising. This has been a sensitive issue among board members, who often have limited personal financial resources. Although they cannot always make large contributions, trustees must recognize an inherent responsibility to contribute financially to their museums. The long-term financial stability of African American museums will be determined by the willingness of boards to take an active role in fund raising. The board must be aware increasingly of the importance of working with the director to raise funds. The growing sophistication of fund-raising methods and the rapidly escalating costs of museum operations have forced boards of all museums to place greater emphasis on money and management than they did in previous years.

African American museums are not exceptions to this trend. If anything their problem is exacerbated by the limited funding currently available to them. While they may be willing, boards often are not equipped to mount the aggressive and multipronged fund-raising efforts that are required in today's nonprofit world. The director must provide both training and encouragement to create the active partnership that fund raising requires to achieve positive results. Without the combined efforts of the board, the executive director, and possible development staff, African American museums will experience limited or uneven growth as they move toward the new century.

The future of black museums rests in many ways upon the enhancement of governance skills at the board level and a strong partnership between trustees and museum CEOs. Leadership must create the rapport between these two central forces that will determine the growth and survival of many of the museums.

## Summary

The history of African American museums in the United States since the nineteenth century vividly illustrates the struggle and commitment of individuals to preserve their history and to build institutions that are indigenous and responsive to their communities. As the museums grew, a number of issues took on greater importance in their determination to survive and to serve their communities effectively. Concerned with contemporary social issues as well as a range of pressing museological concerns, museum directors are seeking ways to secure the futures of their institutions and are pursuing new avenues of support. With the increased number of black museums, fresh assessments are being made of missions, collections, educational services, and financial opportunities. In the process a new level of professionalism is taking hold, and public interest is on the rise. The challenges are significant, but aided by organizations such as the African American Museums Association and the increasing support of African American communities, the path of the future for these important institutions is being determined, and preparations for the new century are already underway.

# 15

# The Multifaceted Role of the Small History Museum Director

by

Charles T. Lyle

CHARLES T. LYLE is director of the Maryland Historical Society, Baltimore. He was director of the Historical Society of Delaware in Wilmington from 1980 to 1989. He has seen previous service in the historical agency field as director of museum properties, Office of Historical Properties, National Trust for Historic Preservation from 1978 to 1980, and as director of the Monmouth County (New Jersey) Historical Association from 1971 to 1978. He was granted a B.A. in history from the University of Minnesota in 1968, and an M.A. in history (Hagley Fellowship) from the University of Delaware in 1971. Currently he is a member of the Board of Advisors of the National Trust.

Museum and Library of the Monmouth County Historical Association, Freehold, New Jersey, where the author served as director between 1971 and 1978. Courtesy of the Monmouth County Historical Association, Freehold, New Jersey.

*T*he role of the small history museum or historical society director is by definition "multifaceted." Whether one operates alone or has a few staff members, the job requires that the director wear many different hats and be the master of many skills and talents. He or she should have academic competence and an understanding of historical methods and materials; a broad knowledge of the various fields that relate to historical society collections and activities; management ability, with expertise in areas such as finance, resource development, marketing, personnel management, and the law; curatorial skills, including technical know-how in registration methods, conservation, and exhibition design and installation; and the capability to understand and handle the multiple requirements of operating and maintaining physical facilities.

Add to this the intangible personal qualities required to effectively lead and move an institution forward, including the ability to work with people of varying backgrounds, ages, and competencies; the self-confidence and enthusiasm to represent one's institution, to communicate its mission, and to attract support for its program; the vision to look to the future and develop short- and long-term strategies to make the institution better; the flexibility to accept new approaches and take advantage of opportunities; the imagination and creativity to develop exciting and meaningful programs and exhibits that will satisfy a wide spectrum of people; and, finally, the temperament and patience to deal with the many unexpected interruptions and demands that are made on the museum on a day-to-day basis.

Most of these qualifications also apply to the large or medium-sized institution head. But there are some major differences. While the directors of larger institutions have greater and more complex responsibilities, they also have more restrictions. The small museum director is by necessity involved in almost every aspect of his or her institution and often is responsible personally for much of the work. The large museum director, in contrast, depends on other staff members to do the work and delegates many tasks through the chain of command. Before major decisions are made, there are often a series of memorandums, reports, and meetings. Then, on the basis of experience and judgment, the director develops recommendations to be presented to the trustees. His or her principal role is that of a facilitator, coordinating and evaluating the recommendations of staff, formulating a position, and seeking consensus. Once a decision is reached the director's task is to provide qualified professional staff members with the tools they need to do the job, to motivate them, to monitor their progress, and to stay out of their way, unless he or she is willing to accept the negative feelings and criticism that invariably result when the director is perceived as "interfering."

Staff members in larger institutions have specific areas of responsibility, and unless they are part of senior management, often have few contacts with the director and board. They generally do not have a full awareness of the pressures that come to bear in the decision-making process and the underlying reasons behind some of the priorities set by the director. While many directors of large institutions are conscientious in their efforts to communicate with the staff and among various departments, staff members usually judge and react only to decisions that directly affect them. As a result, in larger institutions they generally do not have the same concern and involvement in the welfare of the whole organization, and internal politics all too frequently can take precedence over getting the job done as efficiently and effectively as possible.

The small museum provides a different kind of working environment. Relations between the director, staff, and trustees are often kept on a casual and friendly basis. Volunteers are an integral part of the operation and are depended on to fulfill many of the duties delegated to the paid staff in larger institutions. People in small institutions tend to give more of themselves and feel more of a sense of personal identity and shared commitment to the institution and its overall goals. In order to successfully accomplish projects, everyone is often required to pitch in, work together as a team, and share the credit for the outcome. This type of working atmosphere is why so many small institutions become dynamic forces in their communities and why they accomplish as much as they do with limited available resources.

Small museums are more responsive to change than larger institutions. The director who has self-discipline and is willing to put in the energy required to get the job done can have a tremendous impact on an institution. If he or she decides to make an organization go in a certain direction, it will actually move and succeed in proportion to the amount of time and effort devoted and the number of mistakes made along the way. In a large museum it may take years before the director is able to have a measurable impact and longer still before his or her contribution can be fully recognized and appreciated.

While the ability to put one's own personal stamp on an institution is one of the greatest advantages and satisfactions of the job, fundamental to any director's role and long-term success is personal integrity, professional ability, and good judgment. A director must be true to the mission of an institution, understand its history and traditions, and be fully aware of its limitations. A major part of the job is to have the good sense to be able to stretch limited resources on a consistent basis without going beyond the capabilities of the institution and staff. The director who tries to mould an institution to meet some personal agenda or gain recognition will soon encounter trouble.

Along with all of the satisfactions that come with working in a small museum, there are also some very real limitations and frustrations. Small museums never have enough money, staff members, or time to do everything that needs to be done. Every time one major project is completed several more are waiting to be tackled. Small historical societies are often responsible for extensive physical facilities, and something always needs to be fixed, cleaned, or replaced. The director is under constant pressure to come up with new ideas and strategies to recruit volunteer help, attract donors, and expand the programs and services of the organization. But the more successful you are in doing the job, the more people want, the more things come your way; and the more the board tends to take you and your accomplishments as director for granted.

Working in a small museum is never a routine activity. The director and staff have to be prepared to deal with a wide spectrum of people and situations on an ongoing basis. In an average day one can be involved in everything from cleaning rest rooms to fund raising; from dealing with carpenters to meeting with scholars and businessmen; from guiding a group of school children through the museum to giving an after-dinner speech. No matter how well organized you are or how carefully you plan your day, you must be ready to deal with every crisis and unexpected demand that comes along. Whether it is a furnace that breaks down or a trustee who wants you to get something done for him or her before the end of the day, you have to be able to drop whatever you are doing and take the required action. It is not unusual to start a day with the intention of finishing a particular project, and to end it after a merry-go-round of telephone calls, impromptu meetings, and unexpected interruptions with nothing accomplished—only to have to bring the work home with you in the evening.

Carl E. Guthe has probably had more influence on the development of professional standards for small museums than anyone else in the field. After retiring as director of the New York State Museum with twenty-five years of administrative experience in large museums, he traveled around the United States and Canada as a research associate for the American Association of Museums to study the conditions in small museums firsthand. His findings resulted in *So You Want a Good Museum: A Guide to the Management of Small Museums*, published by the American Association of Museums in 1957, and *The Management of Small History Museums*, published by the American Association for State and Local History in 1959. Both are pioneering works in museum literature and have provided invaluable practical guidance to several generations of small museum directors.

In a paper entitled "Our Ailing History Museums" delivered at the History Section of the annual meeting of the American Association of Museums in Pittsburgh, Pennsylvania, in 1959, Guthe argued that small history museums did not in general measure up to what were considered modern standards of museum work. He referred to them as "an ailing element in the museum movement." In characterizing the conditions he had found, Mr. Guthe pointed to, among other things; no full-time professional staff members; inactive and uninterested boards; "slovenly" exhibits; a lack of educational and outreach programs; disorganized financial records; and inadequate collections management. He concluded that small history museums were in deplorable condition and needed professional help.[1]

Since Carl Guthe made these observations, tremendous changes have occurred in small historical organizations. Graduate training programs in museum studies have provided a pool of available entry-level talent, and many small historical societies have been able to afford to hire their first professional staff person. The American Association of Museum's Accreditation and Museum Assessment programs provided a set of professionally accepted standards and goals to work toward and challenged staffs and boards to bring their institutions up to par. Federally funded grants gave small museums the financial wherewithal to implement a variety of important projects. As a result storage areas have been cleaned up and reorganized, collections properly cataloged, important objects conserved, new exhibits installed, educational programs put in place, and newsletters and collections catalogs published. In general small museums are much healthier and more professional today then they were thirty years ago.

I first became a director in 1971 at the Monmouth County Historical Association in Freehold, New Jersey. My career roughly parallels the period of greatest growth in small history museums, and my experiences in many ways are representative of the changing role the small museum director has had to play in order to adapt to new circumstances and respond to new opportunities. When I arrived in Monmouth County in the fall of 1971 to begin work, having just completed graduate school, I had no idea what I was getting into. I replaced a man who had been with the organization for twenty-five years. Typical of many small historical society directors in the 1950s and 1960s, he had been an antiques dealer before coming to the association and continued to run a business on the side. This was an accepted practice and considered to be perfectly ethical at the time, since his salary was so low and the board had so few expectations for the job.

The director and his wife occupied a small apartment at the rear of the museum. While he spent a good deal of his time on the road buying, trading, and collecting for both his antiques business and the museum, his wife opened the building everyday for a few hours, gave tours, and took care of the routine office work. While little was done to advance the organization toward modern museum standards, my predecessor did have excellent taste and was able significantly to improve and expand the museum collections.

My responsibilities at the Monmouth County Historical Association included a museum and research library built in 1931 as the institution's headquarters, and four historic house museums in various locations in the county, two of which were open to the public and two still undergoing restoration. The staff consisted of the widow of the former director, who served as my secretary, a librarian who worked one day a week, two part-time guides for the historic houses that were open, and part-time maintenance and cleaning help. The only allowance the architect who designed the building had made for staff was one tiny office near the entrance measuring about ten by ten feet, which was already occupied by the former director's wife. The remaining space in the building was devoted to exhibition galleries, a small library room, a basement storage area, and a caretaker's apartment. The collections were so extensive and the modest space available so full that there was little or no flexibility. I ended up spending my first two years as director there working out of a briefcase on whatever flat surface I could find.

Although my start as a museum director seems rather backwards by today's standards, I was young, had considerable energy, and was very enthusiastic about the possibilities of the organization. It did not take long before we were able to clean and renovate the basement to open up needed work space and improved collections storage. I spent a good part of my first two years there with a broom in one hand and a paint brush in the other as we cleaned out areas that were jammed from floor to ceiling with artifacts and library materials. In the process we discovered and inventoried treasures from the collections that had not been seen for years. We also eventually were able to take over the caretaker's apartment for additional storage and administrative offices. The extra work space enable us to increase the size of our staff and bring in interns and volunteers.

With the assistance of the Junior League we were able to hire a full-time museum educator and develop an ambitious program for school children that was first manned by the league and eventually by a dedicated corps of volunteers. In cooperation with another local museum, we were able to mount several major special exhibitions that significantly increased community awareness of our organization and its outstanding collections. Building on this community support the organization eventually developed a fine staff, a dedicated group of volunteers, and a wide range of programs.

A number of major developments took place in the early 1970s that changed the character of almost all historical organizations. The National Historical Preservation Act of 1966 was just beginning to be a major factor when I became director. This legislation established the National Register for Historic Places and set the wheels in motion for each state to set up historic preservation programs to assist local projects through grants-in-aid. For the first time federal money was available to small historical societies for major restoration and maintenance projects, and we all rushed to get our historic sites on the National Register so that we would be eligible for grant funds.

Another major change was that grants became available for special projects and exhibitions through the National Endowments for the Arts and the Humanities. While visiting my parents during Christmas vacation in 1973, I filled out my very first grant requests to the NEA to meet a January 3 deadline. Using my father's old Underwood typewriter, I wrote requests for two major exhibition grants and a catalog of the Association's collections. The forms were much shorter and less complicated then. I did not really know what our chances were for funding and hoped that we might be lucky enough to receive one grant. When notification letters came in the mail about six months later, to my great surprise the association received all three grants. I was exhilarated by the news and proudly reported it to the trustees and the local newspaper. What I did not account for at the time was that we would end up spending the better part of the next four years implementing these projects.

With these new grant programs came the 1976 bicentennial commemoration that stimulated historical interest and created a flurry of activity and special projects. We were all swept into working on countless programs and special events and wore ourselves out meeting the demands of coordinating marching bands, battle reenactments, special exhibits, and audio-visual programs. Coming with the bicentennial was a proliferation of new historical societies, many of which started their own museums. In Monmouth County, for instance, besides the county historical society, there were only two local historical societies in 1973. By 1976 there were twenty-eight, half of which had acquired buildings or historic houses. While the celebration helped to stimulate a new interest and awareness of history, it also increased the level of competition.

Another major development that had an impact on small historical societies in the 1970s and early 1980s was the Comprehensive Employment and Training Act, or the CETA program. It allowed many historical organizations to add desperately needed staff from the ranks of the unemployed. Before the act was first passed in the mid-1970s, there were only three full-time staff members at the Monmouth County Historical Association. CETA gave us an additional five full-time positions. It didn't seem to matter that when we were first recruiting people to fill these places, the most qualified person we could find as a library cataloger had never worked in a library before and had a degree in fashion design, or the new maintenance man spent his nights working as a rock-and-roll musician. We needed the extra help. But, in retrospect, the CETA program was a mixed blessing and put a tremendous strain on small institutions. All of a sudden the director had to train and supervise people who did not have the same level of commitment and interest as the loyal permanent staff and volunteers. While the program accomplished some good things, and there are former CETA employees who have stayed in the museum field and have advanced through the ranks, there were also many problems.

In the late 1970s and 1980s museums had to face crucial fiscal and management problems. Directors had to deal with soaring energy costs, less buying power because of inflation, and reductions in federal funding programs. Changes in the tax laws have altered traditional philanthropy, and competition for available funds is much keener because of the tremendous proliferation of cultural and other agencies that appealed to the public or grant-giving agencies for support. In order to survive, directors in the 1980s had to change their emphasis and begin to find new ways of developing sources of earned revenue, memberships, and other fund-raising strategies. Local foundations and corporations have become a key to institutional support. There is also greater emphasis on making trustees more active and involved in fund raising, and organizations often look to the business community to fill board vacancies. Moreover, grant applications to the new Institute of Museum Services are a rigorous and difficult annual ritual for directors, testing their persuasive abilities and writing skills in order successfully to compete for desperately needed operating funds.

With these intensified financial pressures, the role of the small museum director has become increasingly more complex and demanding. The expectations of trustees and the community have also changed, and directors are required to be more things to more people. The traditional emphasis on professional standards, scholarship, and the value of historic resources seem less important today as directors are judged more by their ability to generate publicity and funding than by the quality of the services provided by their institutions.

While demands and priorities of the job have changed and the techniques used have become increasingly more complex and sophisticated, the multifaceted skills required to run and lead a small museum remain much the same. Carl E. Guthe in *So You Want a Good Museum* has perhaps best summarized the role and challenge of a small museum director:

> A director who is respected in the community, who has the confidence of an interested and active Board of Trustees, who commands the loyalty of his staff, no matter how small, and enjoys the enthusiastic assistance offered by an organized group of volunteers, will most assuredly develop his museum into a recognized cultural and educational community agency.[2]

Though written more than thirty years ago, this statement is as true today as when Guthe wrote in the 1950s.

# Notes

**Preface**

1. Leon, Warren, and Rozenweig, Roy, *History Museums in the United States: a Critical Assessment.* (Urbana and Chicago: University of Illinois Press, 1989), xx.

**Historical Prologue**

1. The chief sources for this section are Edward P. Alexander, "The American Museum Chooses Education," *Curator* 31 (1988), 61–80; Alexander, "Early American Museums: From Collection of Curiosities to Popular Education," *International Journal of Museum Management and Curatorship* 6 (1987), 337–51; Alexander, "Charles Willson Peale and His Philadelphia Museum," in *Museum Masters: Their Museums and Their Influence* (Nashville: American Association for State and Local History, 1983), 43–78; J. R. Betts, "P. T. Barnum and the Popularization of Natural History," *Journal of the History of Ideas* 20 (1959), 353–68; Lloyd Haberly, "The American Museum from Baker to Barnum," *New-York Historical Society Quarterly* 43 (1959), 273-87; J. J. Orosz, "Pierre Eugène du Simitière: Museum Pioneer in America," *Museum Studies Journal* 1 (Spring 1985), 8–18; E. P. Richardson, Brooke Hindle, and L. B. Miller, *Charles Willson Peale and His World* (New York: Henry N. Abrams, 1982); C. C. Sellers, *Mr. Peale's Museum: Charles Willson Peale and the First Popular Museum of Natural Science and Art* (New York: W. W. Norton, 1980).

2. James Silk Buckingham, *America: Historical, Statistic, and Descriptive,* 3 vols. (London and Paris: Fisher, Son, &. Co., 1842), 3:374–5.

3. The chief sources for this section are Paul M. Angle, *The Chicago Historical Society, 1856–1956: An Unconventional Chronicle* (New York: Rand McNally, 1956); Julian P. Boyd, "State and Local Historical Societies in the United States," *American Historical Review* 40 (1934), 10–37; Clarence S. Brigham, *Fifty Years of Collecting Americana for the Library of the American Antiquarian Society, 1908–1958* (Worcester: American Antiquarian Society, 1958); Hampton L. Carson, *A History of the Historical Society of Pennsylvania,* 2 vols. (Philadelphia: By the society, 1940); Leslie W. Dunlap, *American Historical Societies, 1790–1860* (Philadelphia: Porcupine Press, 1974); Clifford L. Lord, ed., *Keepers of the Past* (Chapel Hill: University of North Carolina Press, 1963); Stephen T. Riley, *The Massachusetts Historical Society, 1791–1959* (Boston: Massachusetts Historical Society, 1959); Clifford K. Shipton, "The American Antiquarian Society," *William and Mary Quarterly* 2 (1945), 164–72; Shipton, "The Museum of the American Antiquarian Society," in Whitfield J. Bell, Jr., and others, *A Cabinet of Curiosities: Five Episodes in the Evolution of American Museums* (Charlottesville: University Press of Virginia, 1967), 35–48; R. W. G. Vail, *Knickerbocker Birthday: A Sesqui-Centennial History of the New-York Historical Society, 1804–1954* (New York: New-York Historical Society, 1954); Walter Muir Whitehill, *Independent Historical Societies: An Enquiry into Their Research and Publication Functions and Their Financial Future* (Boston: Boston Athenaeum, 1962).

4. Whitehill, *Independent Historical Societies,* 5.

5. Boyd, "State and Local Historical Societies," 11.

6. Whitehill, *Independent Historical Societies,* 8.

7. Boyd, "State and Local Historical Societies," 16.

8. Ibid., 18.

9. Vail, *Knickerbocker Birthday,* 31.

10. Whitehill, *Independent Historical Societies,* 67–8.

11. Shipton, "Museum of the American Antiquarian Society," 41–2.

12. Carson, *Historical Society of Pennsylvania,* 1:5–6.

13. Dunlap, *American Historical Societies,* 73–4.

14. The chief sources for this section are Edward P. Alexander, "An Art Gallery in Frontier Wisconsin," *Wisconsin Magazine of History* 29 (1946): 281–300; Boyd, "State and Local Historical Societies"; Dunlap, *American Historical Societies;* William B. Hesseltine, *Pioneer's Mission: The Story of Lyman Copeland Draper* (Madison: State Historical Society of Wisconsin, 1954); Clifford L. Lord and Carl Ubbelhode, *Clio's Servant: A History of the State Historical Society of Wisconsin* (Madison: State Historical Society of Wisconsin, 1967); Lord, ed., *Keepers of the Past,* 40–66; Whitehill, *Independent Historical Societies,* 243–320.

15. Lord and Ubbelhode, *Clio's Servant,* 178.

16. The chief sources for this section are: American Association for State and Local History, *Directory of Historical Agencies in North America* (Nashville: AASLH, 1986); American Association of Museums, *The Official Museum Directory, 1988* (Washington: AAM, 1987); Boyd, "State and Local Historical Societies"; Dunlap, *American Historical Societies;* Whitehill, *Independent Historical Societies,* 480–98.

17. The chief sources for this section are Alexander, "Ann Pamela Cunningham and Washington's Mount Vernon," in *Museum Masters*, 177–204; Richard Caldwell, *A True History of the Acquisition of Washington's Headquarters at Newburgh by the State of New York* (Salisbury Mills, N.Y.: Stiver, Slauson and Boyd, 1887); Laurence Vail Coleman, *Historic House Museums; with a Directory* (Washington: American Association of Museums, 1933); Charles B. Hosmer, Jr., *Presence of the Past: A History of the Preservation Movement in the United States Before Williamsburg* (New York: G. P. Putnam's Sons, 1965), 41–62, 237–59; Hosmer, *Preservation Comes of Age: From Williamsburg to the National Trust, 1926–1949*, 2 vols. (Charlottesville: University Press of Virginia, 1981), 1:133–82; Ronald F. Lee, *United States: Historical and Architectural Monuments* (Mexico, D.F.: Instituto Panamericano de Geografia e Historia, 1951); Lord, ed., *Keepers of the Past*; Society for the Preservation of New England Antiquities, *Bulletin*, 1–10 (1910–1919); *Old-Time New England*, 11—(1920–); Whitehill, *Independent Historical Societies*, 521–37.
18. Alexander, *Museum Masters*, 195.
19. Ibid., 188.
20. Ibid., 193–94.
21. Lee, *Historical and Architectural Monuments*, 17.
22. The chief sources for this section are Edward P. Alexander, "Artistic and Historical Period Rooms," *Curator* 7 (1964), 263–81; Alexander, "George Brown Goode and the Smithsonian Institution," in *Museum Masters*, 277–310; Henry Watson Kent, *What I Am Pleased to Call My Education* (New York: Grolier Club, 1949); Lord, ed., *Keepers of the Past*; Paul H. Oesher, *The Smithsonian Institution* (Washington: Prager, 1970); Calvin Tomkins, *Merchants and Masterpieces: The Story of the Metropolitan Museum of Art* (New York: E. P. Dutton, 1970); Wilcomb E. Washburne, "Joseph Henry's Conception of the Purpose of the Smithsonian Institution," in Bell and others, *Cabinet of Curiosities*, 106–66.
23. Alexander, "George Brown Goode," 284.
24. Ibid., 284.
25. The chief sources for this section are Edward P. Alexander, "Historical Restorations," in William B. Hesseltine and Donald R. McNeil, eds., *In Support of Clio: Essays in Memory of Herbert A. Kellar* (Madison: State Historical Society of Wisconsin, 1958), 195–214; Abbott Lowell Cummings, ed., "Restoration Villages," *Art in America* 43 (May 1955); Hosmer, *Preservation Comes of Age*, 1: 11–32; Lord, *Keepers of the Past*; Geoffrey C. Upward, *A Home for Our Heritage: The Building and Growth of Greenfield Village and Henry Ford Museum* (Dearborn: Henry Ford Museum, 1979); Whitehill, *Independent Historical Societies*, 461–79.
26. The chief sources for this section are Alexander, "American Museum Chooses Education," 61–80; American Association for State and Local History and Smithsonian Institution, *A Common Agenda for History Museums: Conference Proceedings, February 19–20, 1987* (Washington: AASLH and Smithsonian, 1987); American Association of Museums, *Museums for a New Century* (Washington: AAM, 1984); Kim Igoe, "How to Put Your Museum on the MAP," *Museum News* 65 (December 1986), 19–22; Patricia E. Williams, "The Value of Accreditation," *Museum News* 62 (August, 1984), 55–8. For the International Council of Museums, see UNESCO, *Museum* (Quarterly Forum) and *ICOM News* (Quarterly Bulletin).

**Chapter 2**
1. Paul Gagnon, "Why Study History?" *The Atlantic Monthly* (November 1988), 43–66.

**Chapter 3**
1. National Endowment for the Arts, *Museums U.S.A.: A Survey Report*, research conducted by the National Research Center for the Arts, an affiliate of Louis Harris and Associates, Inc. Under contract with the National Endowment for the Arts (Washington: GPO, 1974), 5. This work states that nearly 40 percent of the total sample were history museums. The number has since increased.
2. *Museums U.S.A.: A Survey Report*, 25–7.
3. Thomas Wertenbaker, "Historic Restorations in the United States," *National Council for Historic Sites and Buildings Newsletter* (September 1949), 9.
4. Michael Wallace, "Visiting the Past," *Presenting the Past: Essays on History and the Public* (Philadelphia: Temple University Press, 1986), 158.
5. George Brown Goode, "A Memorial of George Brown Goode," *Annual Report of the U.S. National Museum, 1896*, 243–4.
6. John Cotton Dana, as quoted in *Fifty Years of the Newark Museum* (Newark: Newark Museum Association, 1959), 12–13.
7. Theodore Low, *The Museum as a Social Instrument* (New York: Metropolitan Museum of Art, 1942), 7.
8. Ibid., 43.

9. Commission on the Humanities, *The Humanities in American Life: Report of the Commission on Humanities* (Berkeley: University of California Press, 1988), 128.

10. Joel N. Bloom, et al., *Museums for a New Century* (Washington: American Association of Museums, 1984), 55.

11. Ibid., 19.

12. Thomas R. Adam, *The Museum and Popular Culture* (New York: American Association for Adult Education, 1939), 25.

**Chapter 7**

1. Near the end of my tenure (1964), the trustees voted to change the name of the organization to the Cincinnati Historical Society; it was my recommendation. The issue provoked a rousing dispute among members, trustees, and the Cincinnati citizenry.

2. At this writing (1990), the Society is planning to move its quarters to the restored Union Railroad Station, near the heart of the city.

3. The MHS is a charter member of the Independent Research Library Association, which was established in 1972 and consists of fifteen major research organizations (e.g., American Philosophical Society, the Huntington Library, the Newberry Library, the Folger Shakespeare Library, the Pierpont Morgan Library, and the New York Public Library).

**Chapter 9**

1. *The American Heritage Dictionary*, 2nd college ed. (Boston: Houghton Mifflin Company, 1982), 947.

2. Karen Broenneke and Keith Peterson, "Planning for Change: How long-range planning can benefit historical organizations of all sizes," *History News* 39 (August 1984), 17.

3. George F. Hicks, "Thinking Ahead," *History News* 37 (March 1982), 20.

4. Ibid., 20–3.

5. Larry Ter Molen, "Preparing a Blueprint for Tomorrow," *Museum News* 61 (November/December 1982), 15–17.

6. Barry Lord and Gail Dexter Lord, *Planning Our Museums* (Ottawa: Museums Assistance Program, National Museums of Canada, 1983).

7. Peter J. Ames, "Guiding Museum Values: Trustees, Missions and Plans," *Museum News* 63 (August 1985), 48–54.

8. Suzanne B. Schell, "Self-Study: The National Endowment for the Humanities reports on its special grant initiatives to state historical societies," *History News* 38 (October 1983), 13–16; "Taking a Hard Look: Strategies for Self-Study in Museums," *Museum News* 63 (February 1985), 47–52.

9. Alice McHugh, "Strategic Planning for Museums," *Museum News* 58 (July/August 1980), 23–9; Robert Simerly, "Strategic Long-Range Planning," *Museum News* 60 (July/August 1982), 20–31.

10. Hedy A. Hartman and Suzanne B. Schell, "Institutional Master Planning for Historical Organizations and Museums," *Technical Report* 11 (Nashville: Technical Information Service, AASLH, 1985), 1.

11. Ibid.

12. Hartman and Schell, "Institutional Master Planning," 2.

13. Ibid., 3.

14. Ibid., 3–4.

15. Ibid., 4–5.

16. Ibid., 5–6.

17. Susan J. Thomas, "The Federal Challenge," *Museum News* 58 (July/August 1980), 31–2.

18. Hartman and Schell, "Institutional Master Planning," 6–7.

19. Simerly, "Strategic Long-Range Planning," 28.

20. Hartman and Schell, "Institutional Master Planning," 7.

21. Ibid.

22. Ibid., 8–9.

23. Ibid., 9.

**Chapter 10**

1. Evening dress is the proper gender-neutral term, but it does not have the same alliterative impact. Anyway I have caught your attention, and that is the first great principle of fund raising. On the other hand the second great principle of fund raising is never do anything that is going to turn off 50 percent of your potential audience.

**Chapter 11**

1. Susan Stitt and Linda Silun, *Survey of Historical Agency Placement Opportunities and Training Needs* (Sturbridge: Old Sturbridge Village, 1974), 100–134.

2. For a full discussion of trustee orientation, see Susan Stitt, "Trustee Orientation: A Sound Investment," *Museum News*, 59 (May/June, 1981), 58–9, 86, 88, 91, 93–4, 96.

**Chapter 13**

1. The Bureau of History came into being as a legal entity by Public Act 271 of 1913 as the Michigan Historical Commission. In 1965 it became a division and is now a bureau of the Department of State. The Michigan Historical Society is a totally private organization located in Ann Arbor and has no official relationship to the bureau.
2. Larry E. Tise, "The Philosophy and Practice of Public History," *The Public Historian* 5, No. 1 (Winter 1983), 44–5.

**Chapter 14**

1. Bettye Collier-Thomas, "An Historical Overview of Black Museums and Institutions, 1800–1980," *Negro History Bulletin* 44 (1981), 56.
2. Ibid.
3. "Afro-American History: Reconstruction to revolt/1877–1977," *Encyclopedia of Black America*, 1st ed. (New York: McGraw-Hill, 1981), 67–9.
4. College Museum of Hampton Institute, Hampton, Virginia. Grant proposal to the National Endowment for the Humanities, 1–2.
5. Ibid., 3–5.
6. Front matter, Bulletin of Research in the Humanities (Schomburg Center Issue) 84 (1981), 137–8, 145–67.
7. David Driskell, *Two Centuries of Black American Art* (Greenwich: New York Graphic Society, 1960), 36.
8. Harold G. Cureau, "The Art Gallery, Museum: Their Availability As Educational Resources in the Historical Negro College," *Journal of Negro Education* 42 (1973), 450.
9. Vincent Harding, "Power From Our People: The Source of the Modern Revival of Black History," *The Black Scholar* 18 (1967), 40.
10. American Association of Museums, *Museums: Their New Audience* (Washington, D.C.: American Association of Museums, 1972), 6.
11. United States Department of the Interior, North Atlantic Region, National Park Service, *Boston African-American Historical Site* (Boston: National Park Service, 1984), 1, 13.
12. Jacqueline Trescott, "Museums on the Move," *American Visions* 1 (1986), 27.
13. Ibid., 26.
14. Ibid., 26–7.
15. Barry Gaither, quoted in Joy Ford Austin, "Their Face to the Rising Sun," *Museum News* 60 (1982), 31.
16. Byron Rushing, "Afro-Americana: Defining It, Finding It, Collecting It," *Museum News* 60 (1982), 33–40.
17. Personal interview with Rowena Stewart, executive director, Afro-American Historical and Cultural Museum, Philadelphia, Pennsylvania. Raleigh, North Carolina, October 1987.
18. Telephone interview with Carole Merritt, executive director, Herndon House, Atlanta, Georgia, August 1984.
19. African American Museums Association, *A Survey of Black Museums* (Washington, D.C.: African American Museums Association, 1987), vii–viii.
20. Thomas J. Schlereth, "Collecting the Material Culture of Black Ethnohistory," *Scrip* 4 (1985), 1.
21. African American Museums Association, Survey, x.
22. American Association of Museums, *Museums for a New Century* (Washington, D.C.: American Association of Museums, 1984), 57.
23. Zora M. Felton, "Black Museums and Education," paper prepared for African American Museums Association, Education Commission, 1986, 2.
24. African American Museums Association, "Education Commission," *Scrip* 3 (1986), 2.
25. Eugene P. Feldman, *The Birth and Building of the DuSable Museum* (Chicago: DuSable Museum Press, 1981), 13–14.

**Chapter 15**

1. Carl Guthe, "Our Ailing History Museums," *History News* 14 (July 1959), 85–8.
2. Carl E. Guthe, *So You Want a Good Museum: A Guide to the Management of Small Museums* (Washington, D.C.: American Association of Museums, 1957), 16.